A Ritual to Read Together

Poems in Conversation with William Stafford

WOODLEY PRESS

ISBN: 978-0-9854586-8-3

Book design by Leah Sewell
        lsewell.tumblr.com

Cover Photo by Donnell Hunter. William Stafford teaching at Centrum, Port Townsend, WA in the 1980s. Courtesy of the William Stafford Archives, Lewis & Clark College.

Published by Woodley Press

The Woodley Press Collection
The Bob Woodley Memorial Press
Washburn University Topeka, KS 66621
http://www.washburn.edu/reference/woodley-press/index.html

A Ritual to Read Together

Poems in Conversation with William Stafford

·

Edited by Becca J.R. Lachman
Introduction by Fred Marchant & Kim Stafford

Contents

III.

Preface

O ver the last year, strangers and family alike have asked me different versions of the same question: How'd you end up editing this anthology? My answer: The Universe nudged me into it. And it's true.

*

My MFA research focused on the intersections of everyday nonviolence and the writing life. I hoped to put my findings into action, particularly as I taught and mentored "the 9/11 generation," now in college. I also wanted to reconcile my own writerly struggles with anxiety and entitlement. Not surprisingly, William Stafford's example surfaced. Connections between his life and mine made it clear that, though we'd never meet, I'd found an important teacher.

At the time, I was the same age as William Stafford when he began his alternative service in World War II, and I also came from a family with close ties to both military service and conscientious objection. Energized by my research on Stafford, I requested a library book called *We Have Just Begun to Not Fight: An Oral History of Conscientious Objectors in Civilian Public Service during World War II*. When it arrived, I was stunned to see the name of my maternal Mennonite grandpa in the table of contents. No one in my family knew the interview existed, and it revealed that Stafford and my late Grandpa Ivan served in forest service work camps just hours from each other. To this day, I wonder if they ever met.

*

I began mentioning William Stafford to writer friends, and it seemed like everyone had a poem about him or inspired by his work. I sought out such an anthology, but none existed. Instead, I discovered in an online search that Stafford's centennial celebration was slated for 2014. *Are you awake?* the Universe was asking me. *Are you listening?*

*

When I volunteered at the William Stafford Archives at Lewis and Clark College (an experience I recommend with gusto), my job was to help document a box of Stafford's daily correspondence found in the attic of his family's former Lake Oswego home. The box was labeled "1980"— the year I was born. Inside, I found letters from three of my past poetry teachers, along with a complex, epistolary portrait of a man who kept everything from rejection letters to invitations to the White House; a former poet laureate who'd respond to strangers' manuscripts via handwritten notes, and who'd offer to dry the dishes if you invited him over for lunch.

The first week of 2013 brought me good news: the 13th publishing house I'd queried wanted to accept the book proposal, and on Epiphany Sunday, no less. So you see? The Universe opened a door, opened many of them; this anthology's simply the result of choosing to walk through them.

*

To echo poet Philip Metres and his reaction to *A Ritual to Read Together*, "this project is, in a sense, a collective memoir of Stafford and his spirit." Because of the choir-like nature of an anthology, it also deliberately plays with the title of Stafford's powerful poem, "A Ritual to Read to Each Other." Its first section responds to William Stafford's use of place, both as location and as an individual's purpose in a larger community. A second section considers the many layers of peacemaking and violence, within ourselves and in our world, while the final section dialogues with Stafford's philosophies on the writing life and teaching writing. Readers will no doubt notice how some poems could span all three sections.

My goal as editor was to feature a wide spectrum of poets at different places in their writing lives, and from both inside and outside academia. Having now spent time with the 601 poems submitted, I'm hopeful those selected can highlight Stafford's necessary, complicated, and dynamic legacy. Most importantly, I hope these poems spark conversations in classrooms and libraries, and at writing groups and kitchen tables. To help encourage this, a study guide includes writing prompts and stories that encourage readers to open Stafford's books alongside this one.

*

Donald Hall ended a recent letter concerning this anthology by saying, "The pacifism never moved from the center of Bill." I've used this as a mantra during the final stages of shaping the book you're now holding. How *does* a writer look injustice in the face, and continue to work with diligence and joy toward a greater good? This is what I want to know. This is what I want to live.

Happy birthday, Mr. Stafford—100 candles is going to make quite a light.

*

In gratitude: For introducing me to the life and work of William Stafford in Early Morning: Remembering My Father, William Stafford, *I thank Kim Stafford. For first inspiring me to teach poetry workshops, I thank the late David Citino. For enthusiasm, support, and guidance at various stages of this project, I thank the luminous Fred Marchant; Dennis Etzel Jr. and Kevin Rabas at Woodley Press; Tim Barnes and the Friends of William Stafford Board; Todd Davis; Jeremy Skinner at the William Stafford Archives; Jeffrey Shotts at Graywolf Press; the writing staff at Vermont Studio Center; and Amy Gerstler. For friendships and long talks about living the writing life, I thank poets Caitlin Mackenzie and Heather Dobbins. And I'm especially grateful to Michael Lachman, for his belief in this book and its editor, and for the wine and chocolate that got me through.*

Becca J.R. Lachman

Athens, Ohio

Worthy Company

One summer, William Stafford's class at Centrum in Port Townsend decided to name their one-week community "Worthy Company," for they were aware of and held a common purpose in advancing the verbal epiphanies of each writer in their circle. In this book, that ritual and commitment live on. Writers and readers in our world are on a rough and challenging road, but they are often in good company, advancing together the idea that imagination, words and poems can make inroads against the dehumanizing violence of our time. Instead of consoling platitudes and aggressive certainties, this "worthy company" believes in the benefits that honest language and humane imagination bring to us all.

One could think of this collection as a multi-faceted letter to William Stafford some twenty years after his death. It's a letter that tells him not only how each poet is faring, but also how important Stafford's writing, ideas, and teaching continue to be. For those who were his friends, it also registers how much his personal presence is missed. But this collection is neither elaborated elegy nor mere hagiography. What Becca J.R. Lachman has done as editor is bring together a set of contemporary poets whose work is "in conversation" with William Stafford. Sometimes the conversation occurs as direct address, other times as vivid recollection, and yet other times as dream vision or ghostly visitation. Some of the poems launch forth from a Stafford line or two, while others pause to reflect upon some aspect of Stafford's life. However, many of the poems make no direct reference to Stafford's life or writing. Instead, they offer us an indirect conversation, often a meditation on some dimension of contemporary life that Stafford himself would have wanted to know of and hear about.

Given the rich variety of poetry in this collection, it's fair to ask: what then does it really mean to be in a poetic conversation with an admired poet from the recent past? What motivates that kind of conversation? Where does it take these poets and their poems? Where does it take us as readers? One approach to these questions might be to begin with the fact that despite a reputation for accessibility, William Stafford was not really an "easy" poet. His greatest poems often bring the reader to irreducibly ambiguous dimensions of experience and feeling. "Ask Me," his best-known self-catechism, ends with him declaring, "What the river says, that is what I say." It's no easy matter having a "conversation" with someone who says he speaks in the idiom of water. On the other hand, one can imagine that exactly such an ambiguous remark might well be puzzling enough to prompt another poet to write in response or to take off in a related but oblique direction.

Echoes of "river-speak" can be heard throughout this collection. Not in a literal sense, but from poem to poem one hears and sees images of the natural world in its mystery: ocean lapping the shore, wind over the prairie grasses, some geese and swallows, coyotes and angelfish, and a new moon breaking into view. There's also an abundance of iconic, evocative objects: hay bales, rabbit hutches, bean vines, yucca trees, the filament-thread of a spider's web against the face. All of these are "speaking" to the poets who write of them. In another poem, we find a young girl bent over a glass case in a natural history museum. She's listening to the "clamor" inside a coral polyp, and recognizing in it some aspect of her own voice. The stance of listening carefully to what the world is whispering is an archetypal Stafford stance, and engaging in that or a similar kind of listening is one fundamental way these poets are in conversation with him.

There is another type of poetic conversation going on in this collection. Consider "Traveling through the Dark," Stafford's most famous poem. Here we witness a person caught in the ethical predicament of finding a dead and pregnant doe on the highway at night, a fawn still alive inside. He needs to clear the road for others, but really does not want to kill the fawn. The poet-speaker hesitates, pauses to wonder what he should do. He says he could hear the wilderness listen as he "thought hard for us all." In that pause, he allows himself to feel all the pulls and tugs that are in fact germane to the situation. This is a poem that dramatizes the enigma and difficulty of existential decision-making. From his conscientious objection in World War II onward through his long, engaged life, Stafford was often in a stance of "solitary witness," and often his most trenchant poems center on his sorting out his responsibilities. Emerging from his daily writing practice, his poems thus became relatively short but genuine, complex vigils of thought. As with Emily Dickinson, a poet Stafford revered, his poems show us a humane mindfulness in action.

Take for example his " A Ritual to Read to Each Other," the poem behind the title of this anthology. That poem likens our lives to a parade of circus elephants. Our connections are tenuous, and we can easily lose each other, and our way. Throughout this collection one hears of predicaments that arise out of our relations with each other. What do we owe to our fellow humans? What do we love in them? What do we fear? What do we hope and pray for that might be better than the world we have? What must we condemn as simply unacceptable? In one poem we find the evening news and war that "tumbles on," and in another we get a glimpse of and a surprising response from a woman in a burqa. We also meet up with a set of instructions for childhood, and elsewhere a report on the ironies of living in "late capitalist society." Turning the pages we meet the Dalai Lama, an analyst, and writing students working at their craft, some of whom are in a state correctional facility. We meet many kinds of muses, and often we touch upon the mysteries of teaching and learning. A number of these poems focus our attention on the misery of warfare and social violence. One cannot say who in this anthology might be a pacifist or not, but these writers never seem to forget that at the core of Stafford's poetry was an ethical and aesthetic commitment to peace-making. A few poems in the collection address pacifism directly, but all these poems and poets want to engage in a conversation with Stafford on how we might live more sanely in our violence-drenched era.

Finally, the poetry collected here embodies an idea of poetic responsibility. Not a grim, puritanical didacticism, but more a modest, collective sense that poetry as an art does matter, that even if it does not save nations and peoples, it can and sometimes does indeed help us respond to the threats we face. Throughout this collection there is a faith that human beings who bring language, experience, and imagination to bear on our problems help nurture human decency overall. Stafford wrote in "Thinking for Berky" that we "live in an occupied country," and that "justice will take us millions of intricate moves." This book collects many such intricate moves. We are in our editor's debt for assembling and editing this prism of voices and poems as one way to celebrate the centennial of William Stafford's birth. We know from his voluminous correspondence that on almost any day, when Stafford opened his mailbox, he would need both hands to scoop out the incoming letters, manuscripts, literary flyers, invitations. Let us imagine now that this anthology has arrived in your mailbox. It promises to be a good day when there's a set of poems like these waiting to be read. In the spirit of Bill Stafford, then, we invite you to sit down with this book and enjoy its worthy company.

Kim Stafford and Fred Marchant
July 4, 2013

I.

Conversation with Bill Stafford

"Well, Bill, what's it like?" "It's about the same. Wind
Is still waiting for human beings to catch up.
You know what it's like—you wait by the car
A while, and finally go on alone."

"A friend of mine died a while ago;
She wrote, 'I'm OK but the food is terrible.'
There's some lack of information here.
Maybe that's why people are so heroic."

"Robert, I can see you're starting out on one
Of your long reckless roads again.
I used to defend you, at parties. I didn't always
Agree, but I do like people to be calm."

"Well, Bill, tell me what it's like." "It reminds me
Of those camping trips we used to take
With the kids. You pack up, but no matter how well
You do it, you always leave something behind."

—*Robert Bly*

The Map

—for William Stafford

Again tonight your words
have come, simple as deer.
And now your moon, snowball
flung by a boy on the last clear
day of his childhood, melts

into paths under my eyelids,
filling those animal tracks
with cold light. I follow
that map, make my way deep
into the forest … until a house

built of pine shadows appears,
a blood-red door, a paned
window where an old woman
leans, dry lips pursed—my name
blooming briefly on the glass.

—Joseph Hutchison

From the Very Start

—for William Stafford, whose first word was moon

The first word your tongue formed
for another's ear
was full as a lighted globe
travelling the dark. Maybe someone
tried to hear you saying *Mama*,
but what you uttered was so deep
at its two-fold center,
the roundness of its saying
left no room for doubt.

A room inside this sound
opened without wall or ceiling,
a passage wide as what your eyes
could take in, thin as a single
gold thread leading you through
each word-swept day. In the sky,
night or day, a glimpse of what
first shaped your breath
still sweeps my breath away—
a ready gleam that's constant
only in endless surprise.

—Paulann Petersen

Black Hills by Day

Time has been a wild horse, twirling leaf, startled mirror.
But there, where the river slowed, my hand was taken by water.
So many birds have flown into eternity while I have been
absorbed with anxiety, allowing the light to fail, without a look.
I have intruded on the sanctity of grief. I have been absent
at the birth of change. For one day in Wyoming, I was able
to stay alone in astonishment. Prairie grasses leaned. Large
animals stood near. Clouds reshaped mountains. The wind
spoke in an ancient voice. I wanted nothing, but more time.

—*Susan Kinsolving*

Big Bend Triptych

1

Cottonwoods

bent over the seep spring
like viejos
wondering what it was

the wind uncovered
and who put it there

a page
from an ancient myth
in need of translation

surely a miracle
to be understood
through the ceremony
of libation

2

Hot

morning sweats with fervor
Droplets
like sin offerings

evaporate into mirage puddles
as believable as salvation
or the serpent's memory
of the garden

Blistered sand
clean as a miraculous portrait
of the Guadalupe virgin
woven by windrift

patiently waits
the monsoon shatter
of pitchfork rain

3

The delicate balance

Santa Elena's shoulders
bunched together
above the quiet river

a dream pathway
for the waxing moon
to carve the letter
of el nombre de dios into sky

above the darkened world
as the river's nubbed teeth
gnaw the slot canyon subway
into granite silt

carrying the great
stone walls
grain by immaculate grain
to sea

—*David Lee*

Lost

The idea of a map is to keep us from becoming lost,
writes the naturalist, now without a chart in the underworld.

The redrock Southwest is like the home of the dead—
dangerous, hot, and bewitching.

Hades is reasonable, and a shrewd judge of character.
He figured brash Orpheus, who knew his way out,

would have to look back. Perhaps he heard
the descending song of the canyon wren.

I like maps, the kind that fold, soften, tear at the creases,
and begin to look like the snowflakes you cut out in school—

a world spread out on your lap as you travel from Crownpoint
to Shiprock. You mark it until the Four Corners becomes a web.

There's a knack for getting lost, says the poet, who was talking
about writing. Just set out—you're better off without a guide.

—*Vincent Wixon*

With Stafford at Centrum

There are people who won't let you be
at home where they live—they
use it up. And places, too,
cities where you can walk a long way
and no one responds to your signal.
It's against the law, or your signal isn't
working—it's a bad day.

I see the lighthouse is still sending
a silvery road into the water,
and I hear that the Sound is still telling
temporary things to the shore. Even
small stones are hesitating to move much.
Time has left behind some beached seaweed
and an orange moon after rain.

I have lived where the sea is in the fields,
where leaves have a rippling look
like water—water farther east, my first town.
So if I call this place "The Long Island of
the Northwest," it means your home makes a sound
I like, right for me. The light slapping
of waves is heard all night where the water ends.

—*Marvin Bell*

Telling William Stafford's Ghost Why I Moved to New York City

The streets are rivers of people,
"unafraid," as you described the water
in the canyon, "of anything but rest,"
and the wilderness is in that breathing river
in the canyon of the steep buildings.

Even there silence can be carved
from the sprawling vista of sounds
by the hard work of listening to what's
blowing inside, like wind against rock,
which gives way, in time.

People and prairie dogs up from tunnels
all blink the same way in the sun,
the way I do encountering your poems,
bright light reflecting off the mica
of shale, cornerstone, hard word.

Anyway, you're staying with me, the lifeline
of your voice. I'll read you out loud
looking down on traffic at the open
windows of my top-floor apartment, that cave
high up on the side of a West Side ravine.

Just ask the pigeons, gusted by your rhythms:
you'll change the air of New York forever.

—*Philip Dacey*

The Noise We Make

that's what the silence meant: you're not alone.
—William Stafford, "Assurance"

We have to learn again to listen
to silences. The way as children we
once learned to see in glimpses through
legs of men, through cornrows, through
the cracks of light in doorways
and sunblind classroom windows,
listen around corridors, through echo and
the engine's thrum—the shush and push
of everything that moves and keeps on
moving through the noise we make
to rise above the noise in chatter, shout, alarm
and siren. We will have to stop our breath
in our throats, our beating blood, our whispered
thoughts and reach past reach far reach out. Faith
itself may be in that last and distant quiet.

—Joel Peckham

What Do You Really Believe

Pray
to
be
useful
as
dead
leaves.

Pray
to
be
useless
as
the
robin's
beak
when
the
robin
sleeps.

—Jesse Nathan

Don't Wait

Starting here, what do you want to remember?
How sunlight creeps along a shining floor?
—William Stafford, "You Reading This, Be Ready"

Starting right here
I want to remember being a very old woman sitting in the park,
I want to remember the April sun on my paper skin
The shock of white hair
That I tuck behind my ear in the wind

Starting right here I want to remember
The evening of my life,
The silver days
Gathered to me like great spools of yarn

"Lean in close and I'll tell you a secret,"
the old woman in me says
"It is all more beautiful than you even dared imagine"

"You are the person I thought I was," she says,
with mischief in her eyes
"Oh I was so busy being me back then!"

"All I want to be now
Is the current under the birds up there
The smell of spring dirt
The spaces where 'I' used to be."

Strange things with meaning
Are happening every moment
Don't wait till you are old to notice.

—*Meg Hutchinson*

Renga

Four geese fly over.
       Appetite pulls the body,
              its shameless honking.

Longing to be loved
       is its own kind of honking.
              Return to the nest.

Here in your grass house
       listen to earth, fire, air
              think about oceans.

All that you can't cross,
       weak, mind full of strategy:
              perfectly simple.

Everything loves you.
       Your mother is everything,
              all of it singing.

Stars along bare branch,
       magnolia or memory
              of wild magnolia.

—*Mary Rose O'Reilley*

Instructions for Childhood

1
Slither solitary as a grass snake
under the fence into water meadows

Share the summer dreams of cattle
grazing on yellow marigolds

Crouch by the track to feel the train's thunder
taste of coal smoke on your tongue

2
A name floats up across half a century
freckle-faced Rosemary with her mysteries

Best at hiding and the most fun to find
she disappeared suddenly, we never knew why

3
That steep hillside forest of fern
will keep you invisible all afternoon

It is all much older than you: the armor-plated
woodlouse, the mushroom, the pebble

And you find every creature makes its own way—
even the paired sparrows settle on separate branches

—*Paul Merchant*

Bringing Things Back from the Woods

Each time I wander into the woods, I bring something back with me. Antlers. Toppled nests. Stones smoothed by streams. The mating call of a wren. (Which doesn't seem to work on humans very well.) Sometimes I return imbued with the attitude of a tree and remain stationary for hours on end. Lately the spirits of the forest have begun following me home. Wiping their feet at our front door so as not to scatter their moss about. Flipping our television on. Bumping against my wife's hip as she chops vegetables for a stew. Testing out the type of rain our shower makes. Rearranging my dreams with their lower branches as I doze. I sense they have instigated a rebellion among our wooden furniture making it nostalgic for the forest. One of our oldest chairs is growing back its bark. A beam that spans this side of the house has sprouted a dozen leaves. And just today when I went to move my desk, it wouldn't budge because its legs had taken root.

—*David Shumate*

At the Source

It is a test for us, that thin
but real, undulating figure ...
—William Stafford, "Spirit of Place: Great Blue Heron"

The Great Blue Heron stands over
the spring, just where its waters
spill out of the earth in winter,
where water trickles in summer.
Bare trees arch over his head.
We watch and wonder how
those folded wings could ever
clear the shelter of this niche.
We do not have his patience,
our hunger for an answer fades.

—Trina Gaynon

Daoist Out of Kansas

Because it was good, we were afraid.
—William Stafford, "Our Cave"

Whatever happened to the guy from Kansas,
that fellow who talked to the grass? Remember him—
the one we'd find leaning to listen
underneath? Or we'd see him scanning the horizon
in the dark. He sure could breathe far.
Had a pet wind in his ear.

Remember when he tried to teach us the flat dance—
plain standing? And that song
for going along your own way called
grammar. Those little handsprings
he wrote every morning helped him master
himself, he said. Nobody else
had the patience, ornery as he was.

Maybe he's really gone or maybe
something else. I keep looking underneath
and listening far. He left us
just enough. Wish he could show us
that cave one more time, though,
and that great fear.

—*Charles Goodrich*

The Last National

No-one to offer lilacs to, none to sound reveille, nobody to name
and no other to do the naming, to call it *October* or utter *chthonic*
in the last of your language, in your olive and old coat, alone
on the range, you fret your arrhythmias and dyspepsias, your throbbing
Manassas and swollen Tuscaloosa, your early tulips tormented
by a belated Noreaster, all your Mississippis draining into the sea,
the parking meters stopped clicking their strict minutes,
but evening materializes still like Kodachrome does in a chemical bath,
night tectonic and glacial, the fortnights unrelenting and rapid,
you think of your spent lovers, their bodies fluorescing
in illuminated precincts, in foreign apartments, how they're naked there
eating mangos and reading Rousseau and need you no longer,
how you're far from the nurturing heart of the tribe,
unable to ring the hours back in their bell or pour the torrent
back in its cloud, unable to reel the errors back to your mouth,
your Buick abandoned in long-term parking, your split-level ranch
a ruin some schoolgirl might grin a hokey grin in front of
in a bright photograph of ruin, in another dead Memphis,
in that abundant future in which she studies your wrecked stadia,
your landfill and essential graffiti, your curious reverence
for neckties and wrought iron and headstones, your blundering
physics, the cute ingenuity of the I-beam and the Snickers bar,
which her people have no word for, the really big God
they don't believe in, how you thought you were singular,
that no-one could know you, but look how capably she clears the earth
from your eye socket, look how gingerly she excavates your clavicle,
look how her hands pillow your jawbone, this little one, your tiny usurper.

—*Jaswinder Bolina*

The Poet's Hand

Inside a diamond of tin-star Kansas
towns—Dodge, Pratt, Great Bend
and Hutch, hometown of the poet who
"came away"—a stretch of pine
and cedar points like a compass
where the south wind said *Go!*
A green sign says *Stafford
County*. It's Highway 50,

and Mackville's filling station is a corpse
by the pavement. Its cracked glass
eyes Edna's Place. The corner
Total Stop replaces both. This week's
banner: "Try our taco wraps."
The old high school announces itself
Home of the Mustangs—only a cemetery
was well attended. Miles east,

Rose of Sharon gives an empty house
red. Her windows are shuttered in black.
On flat horizons, in towns, by roadside
steel tracks, white cathedrals store
a heritage. Wheat. Corn. Milo.
Soybeans. Rigs of irrigation
don't break the cycle. It's
corporations' painting—

landscape by number. The farmer
in a rusted Crown Victoria
drives a road of angles and never
gets home. A small town fades
like the letters *S-T-A-F-F-O-R-D* on a tower

surrounded by sky
—it's the Tin Man's head on stilts,
it's a silver tank that holds

this land's heart. Ground
water. Some say it's running out.
Almost deserted, Zenith hugs
the county line. South
where Ninnescah crosses the boundary,
fields feed river. Cottonwoods rattle.
Once, along its banks, a muskrat
trembled with meaning
the poet's hand wore for life.

—*Terry Blythe*

In a Dream William Stafford Visits Me

He is walking across a field of wheat
in Kansas, grain as tall as his shoulder
and as tan as his face. He is cupping his hands
to his mouth, shouting words the wind steals
and throws into the air like chaff. I need to know
what he's said and begin chasing his voice
as it scuttles across the ground like a sheaf of newsprint.
He, too, is running, but on a slender path in Oregon
cut by the hooves of ungulates. For someone
who's been dead nearly 20 years, he is remarkably fit,
and I can't catch him until he stops at the bottom of the hill
where a stream washes on toward a bay. He says
the sea knows mistakes he has made. He says
the tides have told the world about them.
He points to the sky, and my eye follows
into the tops of these finely needled trees
where darkness and light marry. He asks
for a glass of water, and I realize he is laid out
on our couch downstairs, head propped on a pillow,
left arm bending like a basket to cradle his thick
mat of hair. The lamp on the end table sheds a circle
of light, and he muses about what is hidden
between the pine cone's creased tongues. I stumble
over the Latin for lodgepole, *pinus contorta*,
and tell him this tree must have fire
to release its seed. He is writing on a legal pad
in his barely legible scrawl. I make out the words
let and *fire* and *come*.

—*Todd Davis*

Kansas, Maybe

—for Stafford

Open country, flat, a line of telephone wires
Stitched to the sky way over there. The cluster
Of poplars could mean a ranch in the distance,
Kinfolk, the spread of a certain surmise:
A lawn, clothes stirring on a line to the wide
Will some call wind, a barn, a roan in a corral,
And a few old machines, harrow and plow,
Rusting toward heaven, a place in the ground.

That's as close as you get. You never meet
The man who sometimes climbs into a pickup,
Lights a cigarette, squints a cloud, leans back
And drives out to a field level as living
To fix a fence that holds it all—in and out
With a toothed wire that sometimes sings.

—Tim Barnes

Rabbit Hutches

You'll find them sometimes in those small towns
pushed off to the side by a four-lane bypass
that avoids the boarded up motels and shut-down
filling stations bald in the trees at the junky edge,
those highways gaining a little distance, too,
from whatever's reaching up and out and over—
the steeples, Catholic and Lutheran, the tin-clad
co-op elevator, the water tower with the town's name
turned to the side. Somewhere within a place
like that, propped up on rotting two-by-fours
you'll find a little row of rabbit hutches, three
or four, their doors thrown open, shingles gone,
the plywood floors sour and delaminating,
wire netting torn and rusty, all that's left
of someone's good idea gone bad and left behind,
poor peach-crate hutches hammered up along
whatever might be slightly stronger for a while
until there's little standing but a steady wind,
whining with semis passing on the four-lane,
stirring a little tuft of soft white rabbit fur.

—*Ted Kooser*

Church

This country church
with its one room and steeple,
boards bleached to bone,
endures by the dirt road.

For miles around,
stalks of ripe wheat bow their heads.

Anyone is welcome here.
The last minister had the doors unhinged
and carted away.

Now, white pigeons roost in the belfry.
When the spirit moves, they burst like shot:
a choir of wings, afternoon thunder, angels
into the blue again.

—*Mark Thalman*

Another Visitation

Everyone who hears these words of mine
and puts them into practice is like a wise man
who built his house on the rock.
—Jesus, Matthew 7: 24

Put it on stilts.
—Ms. 1st Century

Old Joaquin's seen the future.
She came to him last night,
one shoulder bare, hair a fright,
sandy-sandaled and ocean-eyed.
He says he came back to tell us all.
"I shall tell you all," he said,
completamente formal,
next morning at the Taquería del Sol.

He couldn't get over how the graceful
young century's eyes brimmed
con nuestros dolores, tiempos, y las mareas—
tides that will not wait, cannot wait
to drown the barrier islands
and creep across the coastal plains
bringing the breakers to La Paloma Solitaria,
turning cotton fields and orange orchards
into salt marshes, arroyos into bayous.
"It'll be sandy soon enough," she told Joaquin.

He sold his truck that very week,
bought concrete and creosoted timbers.
"Elevation's the new salvation"
he'd repeat mantra-like
as he sank shafts through the alluvium

to the bed rock, poured foundations
for twenty-foot piles that soared up
like stilt legs stalking the future
in his pasture's chaparral.

—*Bryce Milligan*

Bale

Immaculate form,
rain-ruined it slumps

rotting
in a narrow

field between fields
of hoof-churned

mud and tramped
stubble.

No animal
will touch it now,

but anyway with days
so cold and ice at night

the animals are gone,
the field empty.

Still the bale serves;
a sparrow

builds up
of drier grass within

a handsome,
deftly woven nest

protected from
the chill and snow;

below, come spring,
a universe

of borers
and beetles

will stir in the damp dark
of its black footprint.

Whether by gale or grapple
the bale will fall

the more upon itself,
ceding shape and name;

this time next year
will be nothing here—

or perhaps just such another
left out as a loss,

as fodder
for the gnashing wind.

To come undone
is the one fate left

to things begun
and forgotten then.

It is why a broken bale
forsaken in a winter field

passed by at speed
and hardly seen

some Sunday or Saturday
can make you cry.

—*Jon Munk*

At the Trough Behind Anderson's, 1957

—a parody of William Stafford's "Everything Twice"

Used to be a dog I remember
a dog I remember used to be
here at sundown, sundown when
you couldn't see but silhouettes
of the dog and the other critters
dog silhouette, and the others at sundown

Once, a bobcat, sneaking out
from the sunglare, sneaking up to eat
right next to it and it bolted
hackles raised and it ran to the sun
but the cats and possum held their ground

I remember. I forget, sure, sometimes
right, but forget it forever I
never will. It didn't mean
much then and the bobcat and the dog
were gone for good, until today
when I remembered them, the silhouettes.

—Ken McCullough

Kansas Grasslands

Big bluestem around us quivers,
alive as horse manes seem alive in wind.
This is the grass Stafford wrote about
as though it were "the sky" or "forever"

only this grass changes colors, mauve
by the Wakarusa River, and yellow,
and by roadside the bleached fox-tail grass.
Grass seed bundles brush against sky,
their long-tied knots loose at last.

We track deer, not Oregon whales,
in these waves, but still we drown
under eight-foot stalks of bluestem.
Switchback grass, too, splays
fronds overhead, like eagle-feather fans.

This imperfect circle is Stafford's horizon,
a curved line to keep stars from spilling,
a quill-stitching through air, a thatched edge—
the path he traveled skyward and back.

—*Denise Low*

The Day After William Stafford Died

There was to be a storm
and the rain came, but
the warning for severe weather
blinked off the lower left corner
of the television just before eleven.
The rain did last into the next morning,
a steady light fall that left
the gardens deeply watered
and the August heat less hot.
After it stopped, somewhere close
to noon, our dog and I walked
down to the lake. I stood where he
had stood, in his steady way.
Our dog did what she always does,
stepped into the water, then ran back
out and sniffed along the shore for fish.

—*Jack Ridl*

Out Where Coyotes Wait

...beyond where the night
surprises the snow.
—William Stafford, "Across the Lake's Eye"

Out where coyotes wait,
and smoke from the campfire
flattens on a lonely wind,

the bare trees bend, clattering
to discuss emptiness—
the sky black above blank snow.

In poetry, they say,
the outer is the inner and vice versa.
It's a lemniscate landscape.

Hear me laughing in the dark?
All I wanted was a surprise
to gallop in unannounced—

An unseasonal tumbleweed of a line,
to bounce right through my fire
and blaze off across the snowfield.

—Jan Hutchinson

Mount Hood Prayer

May the glaciers know they will be safe
beneath these aging memories of blue stars,
who sing new light onto the skins of wild oceans,
where the ghost shapes of whales still remember
their routes, the history of blood still circling their veins,
just like ours, just like the old rivers reassuring the night,
the fire dreams of these mountains, our quiet prayers,
the breathing of every season's first wind—or rain,
this ancient sunrise filling with the eyes of coyotes
and owls, all looking back in a language
that burns deep inside all of our bones.

—*Paul Keller*

Letter to Bill Stafford

Harbor water, but mostly wind
stiffening morning light,
scattering its gray through the empty fish market,
hardening our cheeks,
scraping an empty Marlboro pack
in starts up the Pike Street ramp.

Greetings, you said, have to be worked at
in a city of mornings.

On a local pier I once saw a mate
in wooden shoes without heels,
a Danish sailor watching his men retie
their shoes and load cargo for Alaska.
There was something comfortable in the rain,
the ropes of water on the ramp, and his shoes,
as though he had exhausted
more than a life in them.
One hand hooked in a side pocket
he settled gracefully in his buttocks,
shifting weight like a mountain sheep,
never slipping when he stepped up
the slanted steel to help with his other
hand to roll a barrel on its edge.
All morning it rained. All morning he worked
on the steel ramp, and I heard every step.

—*Leonard Neufeldt*

Cargo

You enter life a ship laden with meaning, purpose and gifts,
sent to be delivered to a hungry world,
and as much as the world needs your cargo,
you need to give it away.
Everything depends on this.

But the world forgets its needs,
and you forget your mission, and
the ancestral maps used to guide you
have become faded scrawls on the parchment of dead Pharaohs.
The cargo weighs you heavy the longer it is held.
Spoilage becomes a risk.
The ship sputters from port to port and at each you ask:
"Is this the way?"
But it cannot be found without knowing the cargo,
and the cargo cannot be known without recognizing
there is a way.
It is simply this:
You have gifts.
The world needs your gifts.
You must deliver them.

The world may not know it is starving,
but the hungry know,
and they will find you
when you discover your cargo
and start to give it away.

—*Greg Kimura*

We Came to a Place

We came to a place
where a deer, grazing beside granite,
  —we could imagine: hunger,
and calm, rush of familiar wind,
afternoon storm, distant
thunder, scent of rain,
shelter under the rock,
a mouthful of pine-shaded grass—
        was blown apart, every piece
of bone strewn across meadow
like jewelry in the rain,
thrown shining into sandy mud,
wet, hot, carrying minute parts
of the deer's last electric thought:
        NOW!
Afterwards, as granite buckled and popped,
and six lodgepoles burned black,
there was no deer.
There was no meadow.
But seeds that need fire whispered
The deer's last spark and began.

—*Teresa McNeil MacLean*

Sustainable Agriculture

Thaw-days, earth-smell, at hand the question
of setting out a garden this year, no mere protocol,
rather an investment in the future of this habitation
whether I stay or no. The soil, cleared in this patch
less than decade, is still the raw red
that sends pines to the mills, scant corn
to the silo or the table. A winter's worth of manure
waits outside the barn's south door, already
a few blades finding the light, experimenting with it
in the new factories of each cell, drawing life
from that rich accumulation. But I am tired
and the wind is wrong, and though it brings a green scent
my heart is stubborn, it will not let itself
be drawn again into the rhythm of the season.
A light rain falls. I had the best intentions.
Without me, nightshade and thistle and the ghost vines
of the melons whose seeds and sweet rinds
we tossed against the hardpan last August, innocent
of endeavor and therefore plunder as well.

—G.C. Waldrep

Bill's Beans

—for William Stafford

Under the leaves, they're long and curling.
I pull a perfect question mark and two lean twins,
feeling the magnetic snap of stem, the ripened weight.
At the end of a day, the earth smells thirsty.
He left his brown hat, his shovel, and his pen.
I don't know how deep bean roots go.
We could experiment.
He left the sky over Oregon and the fluent trees.
He gave us our lives that were hiding under our feet,
saying, You know what to do.
So we'll take these beans
back into the house and steam them.
We'll eat them one by one with our fingers,
the clean click and freshness.
We'll thank him forever for our breath,
and the brevity of bean.

—Naomi Shihab Nye

In Praise of William Stafford

He had one of those faces
I can't remember exactly
it was so plain—
as a wheatfield is plain,
as a lake in sunlight—
and many of his poems
are like that.
They remind me of things
that sometimes I'd rather
forget: the day
I promised myself
I would never be cruel
to anyone, the day
a goldfinch in its elliptical
flight was the most beautiful
thing I'd ever seen. I was young
and usually one keeps such things
hidden. You know how it is.

But sometimes
when the world recedes
it comes back to you,
like that loose strand
of spider web you feel sometimes
in a summer hammock—
momentarily puzzling,
nearly invisible but
connected to something.

—*Ed Ochester*

II.

Twilight

At the end of a day in the tangled
woods of my life,
I step out into the wind
of a hundred startled wings
and wander to a grassy hummock
at the water's edge and sit down.

Soon doves begin
circling back to the wintering oak,
fanning and resettling
to secure their marks
with whatever volition they own
in the wake of a sudden dispersal.

In ones and twos
they glide down to the pond
to drink and to refresh their feathers
with as little concern
as if I were a child of the grass
I'm sitting on.

How lovely
not to be a threat or a *thing*,
to let my fingers touch the water
they've stirred,
for a moment at least, free
from the choices I've made.

—*Dan Gerber*

Hearing the River

There are windows that open and close like steel traps.
—William Stafford, in an interview with Steven Hind

It's a hard gentleness.
Try living
that way, minute by minute,
or even by day.
We live in the mind's
light, dreaming
fields we will never walk
but vow to,
while outside
the current waits.
Sometimes we wake
in the dark
and know the churning
that would free us
from doubt's eddy,
a voice saying,
"It's 4 a.m. Swim."

—William Sheldon

Call to Prayer

It begins in what one imagines as desert but is nothing empty.
For a second or two the air hints at the night we have risen from.

Then the call passes from voice to voice, saying here, this is yours,
take it on to the next, and as if sound could be like waves of the sea,

these gain on one another and grow steeper and louder each time
they touch. The song will overtake dawn at the rim of the valley,

and then enter the old city by the gates of reason, weave through
narrow by-ways piled high with trash no one believes in anymore.

When it reaches the strays that survive, wily and feral, they will
arch their backs, cry out as if in pain, so I might wipe the sleep

from my eyes, rise and open the green metal shutter, and listen.

—Fred Marchant

Burqa

—*London, after the Tube bombings of 2005*

Patriotism is not enough,
I must have no hatred or bitterness for anyone.
                              —Edith Cavell

A waterfall of people trickled down the stairs
and she, beneath a burqa that was flinty,
full of sparks, positioned her stroller

at the top.
The front wheels clunked
like stones towards the station below.

Wordlessly, I unstopped myself
and took the front struts in both hands.
Together, we carried her boy towards the ground—
all of us were once this small,
our bones this soft and compact.

The rectangle of her eyes squinted a smile,
and when I looked back, she waved.

—*Patrick Hicks*

Spring Morning Sampler

—In response to William Stafford's "The Well Rising" and "Malheur Before Dawn"

A pair of swallows
swerve and curve
over the field,
braiding fragrance of lilacs
into breeze,
sun and new grass
into tapestry of light,
their joy
across the fabric of sky,
in beautiful script
embroidering morning
with poetry that
may not save the world,
but reminds me
with every wingbeat,
the world is worth saving.

—Doug Stone

Happiness

—after William Stafford

Out of the darkness the angelfish glides,
Big as a dinner plate. Just a shadow, really, but the tips
Of her wings, even in silhouette, are unmistakable.
And in the very moment I see her, checking me out,
She melts again into the dark.

I've been looking for her
For over a month, in this same lagoon
Where years ago there used to be so many more fish.
Some morning soon I'll come again, earlier.
The water will be clearer.

And I know where she hides.

—Ingrid Wendt

The Given

1.
Wandering at dusk I've found deer
dead, half buried in desert washes.
And I've taken several from the
hollow on my grandfather's farm,
from that thicket of locust west of the creek
my uncle calls the Given.

It is best to drag them up
from below, before it gets too dark,
and easiest to get the truck
and dress them in the barn.

2.
I was a small boy when I saw
in the clearing between the hollow and pines
two bucks with their antlers locked.

They crashed through the brush
negotiating their way along the creek
off the farm, passed the cemetery
toward the high school.

I heard the barking.
A neighbor later told my uncle it was pretty ugly.
Dogs got on the bigger one worse than the other.
Grim, nothing you'd want kids to see.

A year or two later I would know,
facemask to facemask,
gasping through my mouthpiece
that fierce intimacy.

3.
I learned about deer,
then football,
then almost lost a decade of my life to the army.

I've done some swerving,
driving past carcasses without slowing,
stalking the wrong god home.

While I came early to wilderness,
I've come late to learning
how to think hard for all of us.

4.
With my baby boy already walking,
growing strong as a bull calf,
I wish we had Bill Stafford as a neighbor.

That as my boy ages,
he might learn to track the golden threads,
and might notice in the predawn dark
a dim light in the house across the road.

—*Craig Goodworth*

Torture

Her blood is on my hand,
the one that gripped her slender leg,
still warm, and dragged her from the road.
It was night and her eyes still shone
futilely bright for a passing car. They
caught me, looking up as they were
from her reclining, her eyes too late
to see or be seen except by me,
who also gripped her other leg
not yet wet from the blood
flooding where the white
tail of warning had been, her red life
now painting the road behind.
A night class had me driving home
from students who'd fidgeted
at the word "torture," knowing
one definition of the word,
but nothing of its reach.

—*Quitman Marshall*

Untitled Country

There is an odd country, beyond Democracy,
where few live, but many look in and
ask about visas. They say, that country
has no border.

Their flag, the color of wind, never flies
at half-mast. A national anthem,
called conversation, changes
daily, depending on the weather.

That country has no army;
its citizens, even the littlest children,
are allowed to vote
and their votes count twice.

Did I mention? In that country
they celebrate Independence Day
every twenty-four hours,
even in the dead of winter.

—*Scot Siegel*

After a New Moon

Each evening you gaze in the southwest sky
as a crescent extends in argentine light.
When the moon was new, your mind was
desireless, but now both wax to the world.
While your neighbor's field is cleared,
your corner plot is strewn with dessicated
sunflower stalks. You scrutinize the bare
apricot limbs that have never set fruit,
the wisteria that has never blossomed;
and wince, hearing how, at New Year's,
teens bashed in a door and clubbed strangers.
Near a pond, someone kicks a dog out
of a pickup. Each second, a river edged
with ice shifts course. Last summer's
exposed tractor tire is nearly buried
under silt. An owl lifts from a poplar,
while the moon, no, the human mind
moves from brightest bright to darkest dark.

—*Arthur Sze*

Evening News

On the news, war tumbles on.
Protestors fall in the street.
A child comes home

to find her mother,
father, and babysitter dead.
A mother and baby

are diagnosed together.
A sophomore girl is gunned down,
by mistake, in an elevator.

I switch off the television
and step outside. What does it take
to see what darkness gives?

Tonight, it crosses my mind
how gone you are, and stars,
if stars say anything, say Otherwise.

—*Chloe Honum*

Broken Down Car, Bikers

When Kim comes, he brings his guitar, sings,
and when we ask about his father,
   about that motorcycle gang that came in a cloud
   of dust, the Stafford family car stopped,
   hood full of smoke, and that rumble of engines
   and spokes and chrome like pulled
   knives; Kim says father stood
   like a stone, like a monk, like a man
who can say: *Nothing. Nothing here. Move on*,
   and the day clears of its clouds,
and the cycle gang rumbles past. They look,
don't stop. Their taillights glint, blink red.
Their tires pull dust clouds. Gravel like a gnash
of cracked teeth, and the clouds
   follow them down the long road.

—*Kevin Rabas*

Thirty-Two

—after William Stafford's "Fifteen" and dedicated to the 8th grader in the '70s who wondered in class about the point of view of the man riding the motorcycle

I leaned my motorcycle into a curve one summer day
and carried a skid across the road, racing hot
between my legs, the hum and whine of the engine
speeding south across a bridge on Seventeenth
to wherever I was headed. It didn't matter. I was thirty-two.

When I came to, I laid there, stunned at first but marveling,
in a curious way, on my back in the tall grass,
listening to my own breath. A cascade of glistening willows,
visited now with eyes, upward, as though I had just
returned home from a long trip. I was thirty-two.

I imagined I might never move from this watchful spot,
this examined place, this welcome wood becoming me.
Not any road or guardrail now, leaving and leaping
the earth in a forward way with no time to think, no sense
of dread, the beginning of my life. I was thirty-two.

Sensing, closing in, I saw the face of a young boy above me.
He looked as pale and surprised as I must have looked
to him. He took my arm as I sat up, helped me to my machine.
My head ached, there was blood on my hand. I pretended
I was fine, called him good man, thundered off.

I rode away, thirty-two.

—Paul Fericano

Why Empathy Must Be Discouraged in Late Capitalist Societies

According to the latest studies, it all has to do with the mirror neurons,
the ones we can't afford to trust. Look at that face, try not to smile.

Next thing you know we'll be using the word comrade, or wrestling
happily in the mud, or forgetting our lost freedom to throw

the black folks out of town at sunset. For instance, there are cities
in Cuba not named Havana. The island is 1000 miles long,

but only 75 meters wide. Extremity in the pursuit of money is no vice,
but buying insulin for the 101-year old woman who's been part

of the domino game on her front porch since 1956 is aid and comfort
to the Really Bad Guys. Just look in those eyes and say

godless enemy of freedom. You see how dangerous this is. Next thing
you know we'll be taking pictures and talking in whatever language

these people speak, demented or placid, high rise or low.
We'll eat all the arroz con pollo we're offered, smuggle in diapers

if we can, find a place in something bigger, or smaller, than we thought
we deserved. *Indignation without action is froth*, said Gladstone in 1896.

Mix those dominoes, listen to them click and spatter,
take seven. Who's got the double blank? Play it in the center.

—*Jeff Gundy*

In Peace

The Army Reserve recruiter
pitches this line to the high
school kids around his table:
Give us your best,
we'll give you the rest.

I imagine the rest they might get—
flag-shrouded, lined up like
so many kindergarten cots
at nap time.

—*James Dickson*

Ask Her

Some time when the river is ice ask me
mistakes I have made.
        —William Stafford, "Ask Me"

She would have none of it. She wanted
to break under ice to the dark flow
of deeds. *What else is a life but what*
we've done? she wanted to know.

The other students grew quiet,
turned to watch the woman old enough
to be their mother, who'd sat silent
so long in the back of the room.

She hated that poem, and the man
who wanted to cover and run.
And at first I made the mistake
of taking his side. I knew his Buddhist

heart, but not only the kind
wish to be known by inner lives.
For her, no history or "persona"
could salvage the lines.

She fought the current, built
a dam against the poem's seduction.
It was clear she'd had enough comings
and goings, alibis, evasions.

Through her life some father or husband,
brother or stranger must have run
like a molten river. And no pacifist armed
with a poem could make her back down.

—*Mary Makofske*

Briefing Bill Stafford, 7 A.M.

Sorry to say we've had—have—
two new wars since you died, our
longest ever, with at least three
losers. Labor has also lost to greed
in Wisconsin, Davis to the needle
in Georgia. Pols are saying slaughter
in the Middle East is an Arab Spring;
slaughter of Darfuris isn't genocide.
And it appears this president may be
bought, too. Meanwhile, the wind
you say *bends over* never has settled
its secrets, and I'm tired before I start,
my pile of should's stacking up like
dead leaves catching against walls,
foundations. Once I sat in a room
where a beginner's timid lines drew
your no-praise attention, the shy
crinkles smiling from your eyes
a gift, immense capacity to care.
I saw how anything can matter. But
by now you'd have finished your
morning run, written a little something
that might, might not, measure up
to your lowered standards. And Oregon?
Just like my wife said it would be,
biggest rhododendrons I've ever seen.
I felt like her mother, "Suzy, it's so
green!" And all that rain.

—D.R. James

From My Daddy Who Could Not Be Here Today

My Daddy grew up in Georgia
during the Depression. When he was sixteen,
he put on the threads of a U.S. Navy uniform to escape
Jim Crow, moonshine, and those strange things
that happened in trees.

I guess he figured that was the only way
he could stand upright and live life as well
as a *colored* man could in those days. I imagine he was aching
to stop feeling and thinking. He didn't belong to nobody neither,
his Ma gave him up when he was eleven. So maybe he just wanted
to belong to somebody and treated fair and square. I don't know.
All I know is he held on to those threads for nearly 40 years
so Momma and I could eat. Is that what you meant
by holding on to the thread, Mr. Stafford?

Like you said, sometimes whole sides of the world
lean against you, so by some accounts he wasn't
no hero or nothing, he just did the best he could.
But I imagine the two of you could have found nothing
and everything together. You, in your coffers of peacetime
and him, in his war. Sir, I don't pretend to know
the rightness and wrongness of it all. And quite frankly,
I don't understand your meaning in words sometimes.
But it seems to me you both won. There was beauty
in his suffering, Mr. Stafford, the same terrible beauty
you found in the dark.

—*Betty Davis*

Los Prietos

The yucca fans ascend the folded
sandstone cliffs like rows of sea anemones,
memory of when these layers accrued
upon an ocean floor. Funny how the earth
is given to recapitulation, how our own race
repeats itself. I, for example, sitting on this gravel
shore at a long and silent bend in the river,
watching the willow yellow
where it has gone sere and sere before,
thinking about the men who bathed in this deep pool
after a day of building trail, far from the reddening
paths of war, I too a prisoner of spiny conscience,
leaving sediments of self upon this bank,
layer upon folded layer.

—*Paul Willis*

What Were They Like?

—at Cascade Locks, Oregon, site of a Civilian Public Service (C.O.) camp

That they donned metal skins
And sipped the blood of rocks,
Stood a rain that could unzip
The body to shadow and bone—

Yet at the bottom of the gorge,
Beneath the rubbed topography
Of crabbed evergreen and stone,
In a time of seamless war,

A barrack hunkered under snow—
Closed, dreaming, ravenous,
Where they would daily slough off
Sleep, climbing out of what they knew

Into some circled unharmed thing, words
Brushing fingers against gritted lips.

—Philip Metres

In Memory of Bill Stafford, Good Indian, Who Fought to Save Crow's Feet's Band and Other Survivors

Alone, and armed
with a peace pipe, he
was scouting the enemies in
his genes, and in
the centuries of English history's
colonization of each new American generation's minds in
universities, when,
after winning all the Indian Wars
he could, by losing the parades,
he found himself
leading more brothers and sisters than he
or anyone on this battleground,
our society, had thought
alive. Completely, wholly, surrounded, he fought,
as the young pacifist he'd been had fought, with
and for everyone, by giving Up
and Upside-Down
and, above all, Always
Beyond-bounds, a second, a third
and, yes, an infinite chance, until,
summoned by Sun—
for council, accolade, well-deserved rest
or who knows what—
to our mind-freezing sorrow our words try
to insulate out, he went.

—*Ralph Salisbury*

Equilibrium

In Sacramento, I was a newspaperman, but now I stuff
newspapers into cracks around the doorframe, between
the floorboards and into knotholes to keep sand, wind
and rattlesnakes out of our barracks.

Here at Topaz, the Jewel of the Desert, I have become a carpenter.
I use my hands to make life in the camp bearable for my family.
When we arrived, our shack held nothing but four army cots.
For mattresses, we were given bags to be filled with straw.

I salvaged lumber from the yard to build crude furniture—
a table, chairs, and a few shelves. Emi borrowed a broom and
swept out the dust, then sewed curtains by hand to hang in
the window. My son made a pull toy from the lids of tin cans.

Mama came with us. She was an Issei and a poet.
One day she wandered into the desert and never came back.
I fashioned a box with no nails to hold her ashes.
Emi made an ikebana from tumbleweeds.

Beneath the shadows of barbed wire, I have discovered
the beauty of tools. How a plane can subdue the harshness
of wood, its cold steel a comfort in my palm. How a level,
with its bubble that does not freeze in winter, can offer levity.

I have learned how to face a sandstorm with a strip of cardboard
plastered with glue, then to use this sandpaper to smooth out
the incongruities of our lives. I have been shown the miracle
of precision and balance—how a hammer can straighten out
the bent backs of nails and make them useful again.

—*Margaret Chula*

Peace Vigil

In the park our circle of lights grew,
passersby drawn to its silence in the deepening
dusk. The dark spaces between us filled in
with candle-flames cupped against the wind.
In the center we did what the government
wouldn't, invited Peace, and she appeared.
A young man, cannon fodder age, shouted
from his truck, "Fuck you! Bomb Iraq!" Our
silence bent but didn't break. We stood
in a place of skulls. Mostly sadness
for the poverty of it, the smallness
and "pity of war." But anger too,
reminding us that the war is inside
everyone now, a war we must be
prepared at any moment not to fight.

—*Thomas R. Smith*

Rationing, 1945

What stays massed in the mind
are instructions: render the fat,
reuse the tea; save, sure of the reason.

This was dread:
hardened, and solid as lard.
Grudges were holstered or held

to the light, their milkweed dispelled.
The sponge was wrung for its last.
We went together, washed and chagrined,

to wait for the cans, contents unknown.
Intent and covetous, lit by hunger,
we opened them, and complaints

disappeared in our mouths.
We went together at midday, at dusk,
to seize the fuel, the flour—

as some mother went weeping
against the wall—
to seize the milk, which was ours.

—*Joan Houlihan*

Weight of Water

Four tweets inspired by William Stafford

Do you know the weight of water?
Carried on the head for a mile?
Sprayed by cannons?
Scooped to wash the bodies of your dead?
#stafford

> Coffee: never bitter at 9,
> sweet red beans plucked;
> its aftertaste came at 15,
> learning the meaning of famine
> &cash crop in a day.
> #stafford

St. Luke's down the street:
didn't go this week
to ask: "Rev., who wrote
Numbers 31
1 Samuel 15
Deut. 0: 10-14?"
#stafford #Iraq

> "Mama, how can I be your Freedom?
> And did you know you are my Freedom?"
> At 6, he grins&skips&spins
> As I learn his radiant lexicon.
> #stafford

—*Christina Lux* (@ca_lux)

Villanelle for William Stafford

It should be something easy,
should that word to watch for.
A word that's easy

to use *and* misuse. You'll agree,
or disagree, that *should* is like *more*—
it *should* be something easy,

but maybe not. More or less, we
live our lives before
words that are easy

to mistake: work, family, country,
love. We come and go. It's either or.
It should be something easy,

shouldn't it, *it* being the tree
to climb, the brush to clear, the four
words that are easy

to line and break: *How to free
ourselves*? To open that door—
it should be something easy—
one word. And then the next. Easy.

—*Ken Waldman*

Breathing in Wartime

Glass magnifies two bulging pupils:
a goldfish peers beyond its bowl,
perhaps as far as the windows

of the next building
where a man in dress shirt and tie
appears, gathers papers from a desk, disappears.

The fish makes o's with thin, gold lips,
stubborn little o's I mimic,
opening and closing my mouth.
Repeatedly reflected in the windows

where the desk remains vacant, a jet
ripples, shrinks and stretches,
tail fin catching the light,
the spikes of a silent explosion.

—Derek Sheffield

Political

There was a war going on, though it never seemed to intrude the way we thought it should. It reclined in the background of life like the mountain looming behind the city, and I never really thought about it. Instead I thought about how I should be thinking about it, and I worried about *that* but it wasn't really a big deal. I wasn't going to be drafted and people were going to die whether we stayed or whether we left and the *we* in our *us* was something less than inclusive of me so I was like "I don't know what to think." Although I did have an opinion. I just didn't know whether I was right, and if I mentioned it to someone, they might say "Well have you considered *this*," or "You're being too polemical," though the latter wasn't really a problem since everyone I knew agreed with me, which made me suspicious, since we'd never been right about anything before, or agreed on much except that life was difficult but mostly good, and we came out in favor of beauty, and generally agreed in principle that killing was bad. Everyone knew that anyway, which meant everything *not* already known felt unknowable, and if you did know it you couldn't change it anyway, so we raised our glasses to the troops, and we raised our glasses to the new candidates, but to be perfectly honest we were going to raise them anyway. It was our way of saying "Enough!" which was our way of saying "Perhaps if I ignore this long enough it will go away on its own" which was our way of saying "You intrude so readily, my dear, but I wish simply to have a small nap and then perhaps some tea on the veranda" and that was a platform finally we could get behind.

—*Robert Cantoni*

Things I Learned at Sixty-Six

—after William Stafford

When you let your breath out
you can reach farther.

Some rocks look solid
until water dissolves them to sand.

A tiny piece of paper partially pushed
by thousands can elect the wrong person.

When Anna's hummingbirds hover in sunlight,
red feathers turn iridescent green.

The last measure of Handel's "Messiah"
can trigger tears.

Snipped cilantro overtakes the smell
and taste of everything it touches.

Waxed intrinsic thread slides through brocade
easily and holds for a hundred performances.

If words leave your tongue without screening
through your heart, you'll be sorry.

Juice of Suffolk Red grapes can jell as clear
as Christmas cellophane.

When they get old, some people lose their selves
before their bodies die.

—Patricia Wixon

Bare Spots

I scatter grass seed—
some for the lawn, some for birds.
The large bag allows for failure.
If wind told time, each seed would be a second.
If memory grew, it would grow like this.
If my extended arm were a wing, I still
could not fly. I scatter the seed,
and the blades beneath me
bend, and listen.

—Jim Daniels

The Pine Marten

—in response to William Stafford's "Chickens the Weasel Killed"

Last winter I laid my fishing poles
on the roof—strips of herring strung
on circle hooks—and left the baits
to freeze for the night. In the middle
of sleeping, there were footfalls
and then the sound of small stones rolling.

A pine marten tried to carry the herring away,
but cumbered with rod and reel, he took
to eating around the hooks. Back then my urge
was to destroy the marten, a nuisance, a nasty
annoyance. But now I leave gifts, small prayers
of meat in fine rows along the roof's edge.

In the morning, when I read the writing of his prints
and see the offerings accepted, my soul rises.

—Paul Brooke

At 4 A.M.

an excerpt from
I Love a Broad Margin to My Life

                                    At 4 a.m.

the Dalai Lama and William Stafford are awake

with me, and meditating and making up

a poem, and making up the world, preparing

the morning that we can

live as peaceful, gentle,

kind human beings. We build the Kaya,

the Body, and the Dharmakaya,

the Buddha-body. Hold our bluegreen

world joyous and vibrant.

—Maxine Hong Kingston

Freeing the Dead Cow in the River

In the daydream poem-to-be that surfaced once years ago
it would have been a woman, her last slow float down the river
in the final grip and current of her one life story,
and I, on the bank, would have sighted her and dreamed her
a song, perhaps her first, perhaps only her last;
I'd have thought for us all, then chosen the wisest nothing,
let her go on alone, as she seemed to know how to.

This thing snagged here instead, the ineluctable
cow conferred by the only and endless world—
just a distended black-and-white hump above water,
far too much like a hugely pregnant belly;
the rest furred brown, as if she'd been long on her way.
I let her be for a week; she was getting nowhere
till I gave her a first timid push with the end of a garden rake.

I wound up good and wet in that bad Ganges,
fell in, at first, for trying too hard to stay dry,
then waded in with the rake to muscle the bulk of her
free and nudge her out like a tug to the channel.
Her head rose out of the water once, pale and rancorless;
then she found the current and it took her
and I who'd freed her turned to my next labor.

—*Eric Torgersen*

Catbird

The catbird fanned his tail in May
the way a man strums his half-tuned guitar,
string by string. Then he began to sing
his song of songs: borrowed notes,
phrases lifted from the public domain.
Thank no one. Pay no one.
Soon she came fluttering to the wire,
slender and gray.

In May you cut your winter-long hair outside,
silver trimmings on the wind.
The catbirds made their selection,
lining their tinseled nest.
Eggs appeared, a sensible two.

Just two. And the singing ceased
in favor of secrecy, stealthy
comings and goings in the honeysuckle hedge.
Why do we regard all this as instinct?
As opposed to what? Reason?
Why did we have children?
Because I suddenly wanted to.
That was our reason.

One day you came through the open summer door.
"Something terrible has happened."
You had found a half-fledged chick
drowned in the rain barrel
and pulled it out with a clothespin.
A few days later the other lay near the driveway,
its tiny beak swarming with ants.
That's business. That's capitalism.

And from the center of the hedge
the mother called to them all day,
and again all day, and again.

I listened as I pollinated squash blossoms
with a watercolor brush.
Where were the bees this year?
She sang in a minor key,
and I took it personally. Sometimes love
seems just another word for work.
But we can't let that stop us.

That same summer weddings came to pass,
and divorces. Homes stood empty.
The chances were never quite fifty-fifty.
But for scavengers, the odds were better.

—*Connie Wanek*

The Price of Right

*So much grace available, but how we receive it depends on what
we can let go of.*
—Joi Sharp

Inside the place where we are right, the rain
can never fall. Inside the place where we
are right, the leaves fall yellowed off the trees.
No breeze. No bells. No peaches. We explain.
We judge, contend, defend and claim, maintain
our certainty. And meanwhile, we don't see
the lilacs wilting, grasses browning, bees
without their hives, lost crows, the sunset drained.

But sometimes in this shrinking cage of right
wings in a doubt. A question. Nothing's clear.
And see how soon the crows return, a slight
of breeze, a scent of rain. I'll meet you here,
this open place, exposed, unclosed. How light
spills in as our defenses disappear.

—Rosemerry Wahtola Trommer

That Certainty

People think they're good because
somebody hit them when they weren't.
They say, *Ya gotta teach em—*
dogs or kids—*how else they gonna learn*?
I don't answer, never have known how
to say, *No, you'd be good anyway*.
I'm sure of it.

That certainty—I'm right,
you're wrong—is what somebody
hit them with a long, long time ago.

When I neither argue nor agree,
they glance at me, then look away,
and back, and in that flash
before our talk moves on, I see
the child in that moment
just before the slap, the fist,
the tongue-lash taught them
they were bad, they had to learn
how to be good.

—Helen Frost

Embers

I hesitate, the hour late,
in a quiet landscape while one son watches me
        from the shade of a tree,
and one son waits, hand raised to shade his face

        on a path that is hard-packed,
the grass beside it trashed; a place more windbreak
        than woods, more clearing
than campground on our first outing in years.

        Still hot, not yet fall;
the brush dry, a hint of red in leaves
        that scratched the side of the tent
when we went for something to burn

        as if I needed a fire
when alone with these men, I remember them
        as children who played so close
to the smoke and embers that I slapped them

        hard enough to make them stay
at a distance, and felt justified until they hid,
        and I heard a boy crying;
shirt torn, face scratched when I found him

        in the brush with his brother
who held a stone in his hand, and I knew
        I was not going to tell him to drop it.

        Whatever I did or did not do
brought me to this moment, and I stall for time,
        more time to find them again.

—*Warren Slesinger*

At the Stafford Stones in Foothills Park, September 11, 2006

Thousands of years Indians lived here
but today a man walks his golden retriever
as kayaks instead of cedar canoes
navigate the mighty Willamette.
Kids in the nearby wading pool still gift
a sunlit baptism on all passing by.

—*Scott T. Starbuck*

At the State Correctional Facility

"We're going to find words," they tell Security
as I lead the English class of ten, minus one locked-down
today, outside to observe the trees. Write down everything
you can, I say, and they go at it eagerly, not questioning,
perhaps, the odd ways of a poet. Plus there's sun and
breeze today, we're at the center of this green campus;
we can't see the fences from here. The kid with THUG
LOVE on his knuckles says his tree is cozy. All those shabby
leaves like fur. We find loser trees and confused trees.
A patrolling car on route stops by to say hello. There are
things far worse than winding up at juvie. Like, possibly, not
stepping out, not coming here at all. The ash the class has
gathered round is "dull—not climbable," says THUG LOVE.
We count the limbs sliced off, we puzzle at its cinched-in base,
chipped by the careless mower. All these guys have been addicted,
who knows who has been abused or what they have inflicted.
They sit on the grass, all uniforms and sculpted faces,
not "fixed" and attentive. About the ash, the boy with doll eyes
says, "It looks like the kind that just takes it and takes it silently
until one day it snaps." Scared to read them poetry, I stall
until there's time for just one, then read to them of ocean.
All nine listen, eyes fixed, still: young men who see everything,
who see, who want to look.

—Emily K. Bright

His Blessing

This hot July noon
       he wears chocolate jeans
              and a pearl-buttoned shirt.

As a courtesy to the sun
       he tosses his denim jacket
              over the hydrant.

In accommodation to the weather
       his pseudo-Stetson is straw—
              not brown felt.

Unfailingly smiling and waving,
       our cowboy sits on a stone wall
              near the edge of town

where State Rte. 3 crosses Ella.

For visitors,
       he is the first welcome to our town—
              kind, giving, living in some
                     otherwhere.

All of us receive his blessing—
       I am ashamed it took me so long
              to wave back.

—*William Reyer*

Last Class

How can he explain what it was like?
Towers and people were falling, dust
swirling, glass crunching underfoot.
Most amazingly, the sky was missing.

What it was like, he supposes, is like
what it is when he wakes up at night
and lying fixed at absolute zero sees
there never had been any wings to melt.

He takes down the Shakespeare poster,
puts Wordsworth in a box, and closes
the office door. What a cosmic oddity,
the timing of a universe. What a clock.

—*George Drew*

Some Beliefs About Mountains

I believed South Mountain made all things
beautiful and good.

I believed all the world was safe
except wars and dogs.

I knew the weather drills were really Russian drills—
we never saw tornadoes in Cumberland Valley.

The day the airplanes dove into New York and Washington,
I crossed those mountains.

—*Travis Poling*

Forgiveness

Something will tell you, 'This is it! Eureka!' If you still feel lonely in your heart, or bitterness, you'll know that you're not there.
—Anthony, in Jonathan Kozol's book *Amazing Grace*, describing heaven

If you feel bitterness leave your heart,
it will float lightly in the sky like milkweed in a blue wind.

If it floats in the blue wind, other people will see it float by
and think that it is a thing of great ethereal beauty.

If it's a thing of ethereal beauty, it will float in the air
for a long time before it falls to earth.

If it falls to earth, it will bury itself in last year's decay
and return as a green shoot in spring.

If it returns as a green shoot in spring, it will grow into something beautiful,
as if it is a tree in the kingdom of heaven.

If it is a tree in the kingdom of heaven,
all the birds of the field will come to roost in it.

If all the birds of the field come to roost in it,
then they will begin to sing.

If the birds begin to sing all at once they will fill the dome
of heaven with their song and it will echo off the canyon walls below.

If it echoes off the canyon walls below, then we
will hear it and it will enter our hearts.

If it enters our hearts it will move through our bodies,
like a leaf floating on a stream.

If it floats like a leaf on a stream, it will be like an empty vessel
waiting to be filled with what we choose.

—Stuart Kestenbaum

The Message & William Stafford:
Cento

I will tell you a strange thing.
I looked back when I left.
God guided my hand.
I hear a room open behind me
A secret storehouse that saves the country.
And I stand here, home-come, to celebrate,
Feeling at rest, all danger gone.
When you send messages they come spinning.
This is your time, your world, your pleasure.
I will listen to what you say.
(You don't ever let go of the thread.)
Go ahead. Tell us. We're listening.

—Kathleen Gunton[1]

[1]Line 1 - "Report to Crazy Horse"
Line 2 - "At the Klamath Berry Festival"
Line 3 - "Vita"
Line 4 - "Existences"
Line 5 - "Waking at 3 A.M."
Line 6 - "Homecoming"
Line 7 - "Glances"
Line 8 - "Elegy"
Line 9 - "Godiva County, Montana"
Line 10 - "Ask Me"
Line 11 - "The Way It Is"
Line 12 - "Slow News from Our Place"

*All poem titles above by William Stafford.

III.

One Morning We'll All Awaken without a Theory

at wooden desks,
our blank composition books
exuding their distinctive freshness.

Not translation
nor transliteration—
heaven forbid
"original work."

Like the abbots of old,
our first-grade teachers knew:

there is a rest that comes
in copying by hand.

The breath unclenches.
The heart settles quietly into itself.

On the blackboard, swathes of erasure,
backwash of the cloud
that must have passed through
while we were dreaming.

—*Claire Bateman*

Girl in the American Museum of Natural History

The next case shows how coral
is a bud producing rock, like a mouth
whose teeth are on the outside,
or a body within a bone.
It moves by growing.
The girl keeps her ear pressed to the glass display case,
listening for the clamor
inside each bustling skeleton.
She can see now her own voice
is a polyp and when she shouts
whole new colonies of sound echo back.

—*Laura Smyth*

Eating Tacos on the Curb with William Stafford, May, 1993

After your morning's workshop when you leaned
forward into our words until they fell into place,
the least I could do was buy you lunch.
All the restaurants closed for *Cinco de Mayo*,
booths and Mariachi music lined the streets.
You asked what it all meant. A good excuse
for a party, I said, victory
over some battle or other. You smiled
that famous smile, sort of like a comma
resting on its back and we settled on a taco
stuffed with chicken, extra salsa. Some water.
We sat on the curb shoulder to shoulder
looking at a sea of feet, me not believing
my good fortune. With drips and slurps,
the subject was finding our poems a home,
a struggle for even you, your admission,
advised, *remember, they need you to stay in business.*
You took another bite. *And have a good title.*

—*Perie Longo*

When you can't find the poem

you want, the one that travels
out to the frozen river

at dusk, and listens
for the first crack

of ice breaking
apart, revealing veins

of pewter and white
in the dark, that moment

when meaning opens, a current
under the rigid surface

loosening, beginning to pull
the world along

into the first days
of spring, into the question

that answers everything— *seems*
to answer everything—

when that poem
will not be found, you must

celebrate its small life
with another.

—*Wendy McVicker*

Drought

What you do, you wait for a great drought to end.
Even if by then the stalks are gray
and the buds crumbling—day
by day, wheat so stiff
it breaks in your hand. And when
you look to the sky for rain,
you find no friend. Old friends
are best, they say. Then again,
the hungry stock need hay;
they're near the end. And the end
looms in the interminable haze
of unending noon and sun-drenched days.
So you wait—feet on parched land,
eyes on the sky, and an upturned hand.

—Ed Meek

Start Close In

Start close in,
don't take the second step
or the third,
start with the first
thing
close in,
the step
you don't want to take.

Start with
the ground
you know,
the pale ground
beneath your feet,
your own
way of starting
the conversation.

Start with your own
question,
give up on other
people's questions,
don't let them
smother something
simple.

To find
another's voice,
follow
your own voice,
wait until
that voice

becomes a
private ear
listening
to another.

Start right now
take a small step
you can call your own
don't follow
someone else's
heroics, be humble
and focused,
start close in,
don't mistake
that other
for your own.

Start close in,
don't take
the second step
or the third,
start with the first
thing
close in,
the step
you don't want to take.

—*David Whyte*

Picking and Choosing All Along

That's the beauty of it: you *can*
write about that summer day, you *can*
write about that war, and you *can*
write about neither nor anything else
for the moment, for the day and days.
Heat your lunch in the microwave
and set a place at the table, by the window
looking out at the circle of bricks
the hydrangea has married in the middle.
You *can* let that poem wander the streets
until it comes to the realization
that it's been looking for you, alone, all along.
Make it work for its keep, its magic.

—*Tim Suermondt*

Taking Advice from William Stafford

To wake up without a fire at five in the morning
before the sun and my sons wake, to climb

into my page, to absorb the city I grew up
in, to listen for what birds are

as anxious as I am, to follow that golden thread,
that flicker, to do my work, for real, listening

deep for every thing,
to write, to spark—

—*Dennis Etzel Jr.*

For You Who Stopped to Read This Poem Posted Outside Our House Because You Thought It Was an Ad for Real Estate

"Oh, it's only a poem," you say,
not realizing that another fenced yard
isn't really what you're looking for;
that more or less square footage
will never measure up to coming home
to where you really live.

True, there is no market value here,
no closing costs except those incurred
by what you've refused to let in or out;
no interest accrued apart from
your ongoing willingness to read.

See, even now, what a hard sell it is
getting you to step beyond
the threshold of all your wanting
back into your own house,
back into all those rooms inside yourself
you have yet to discover,
the limitless living space of your heart's
red-velveted chambers beating quietly
behind every door.

As if something more real than real estate
were inviting you to move in
to wherever it is you're standing.
As if the walled-off poetry
of your own life were knocking
to be let inside.

—*Daniel Skach-Mills*

Compliments and Complaints

—remembering Bill Stafford

"I tip myself on my side
so the words can flow easily."

I tipped myself as well,
sleep came easily.
So I sat and scribbled,
emptying the wrong words
from my pen
before forming the good ones
into lines.

I would bring him 'my stuff'
timid or with masked exuberance.
Either way it was
the same game every time:

I was blindfolded,
Spun around three times,
Sent to make my best guess,
Did I get the donkey's ass?

His answer was always the same—
"If you like where you put it...
then so do I."

—Peter Quinn

If a Tree Falls

A tree fell across the yard last month,
missed the house, and dropped in the wooded lot
next door. Maybe it was only chance,
a hundred sixty foot Douglas fir,
twenty-two inches through, falling;
it didn't damage anything, but left
its exclamation point across the lawn.
Somewhere, beyond Orion's three-star belt
and Cassiopeia's topsy-turvy chair
a celestial engineer must have aimed
a puff of cosmic wind just as straight
as a cyclotron particle or laser light,
a perfect line in geometric space,
and the tree went down just as it should.

—Shelley Reece

Charms Against Writer's Block

Make a novena, a devotion to the gritty wanderlust
that bites the soul: nine straight Friday midnights
at the Greyhound Bus Station, feeding coins
to the television, avoiding eyes of the police.

A clear night, walk outside. Look up. Note
how little you mean alone, how skin glows with light
it took all time to make this earth, how holy you grow
by wondering *where* and *when* and *why*.

Stand naked before a mirror in bright light for one hour,
trying to take yourself seriously; trying not to.

With a lover at the moment of *O my God*,
look together into a mirror to see how, for good and ill,
passion transforms what you are.

With friends you'd trust your nighest hungers with,
those whose words you treasure, carefully, lavishly
prepare a great feast: meat, herb, root, salt, fruit,
a little too much wine. Sit at table for three hours,
silent, touching nothing; then go out
and give everything to the poor.

Lean over the bed to catch the last breaths
of your mother and father. Take them to heart.
Speak nothing but the truth about the dead.

Decide what to do with your hands.

Recalling Mallarmé, that "there was within him
that which would count the buttons on the hangman's vest,"
study Death's outfit as he tightens bony hands
around your throat, the way he wears his hair.
Stare down your dank fear, your fragrant desire.
Breathe and breathe the song of your life.
Let nothing get by you. Write it down. Again and again.

—David Citino

Work

What will you do with important things in your life that nobody notices?
   —William Stafford, "Waiting for Poems to Come"

Like the return again
and again to attention,
to being in my body,
seeing through my eyes,

stepping in my step.

Or forgetting to. Lost
in a haze of thoughts.
The slap of the door on my fingers
brings me back.

When I lift my hands to the steering wheel,
when I look out at my class at the start
and ask, what feels right?
When I find my breath caught in my chest,
I return. I return.

—Sarah Webb

Ten Years After the Last Words

Ten years after my father, as he helped my mother
clean the kitchen when the blender had exploded
scattering lime pie filling everywhere, said,
Better get another spatula…
and then fell dead to the floor,
I was standing at the wall with the sheetrock trowel
buttered with finish mud to cover the dimples
of the nails, the panel seam snug against the stud,
and I asked my father in my mind, "Daddy,
have I done enough for you?"

His voice bloomed in my mind:
Years ago. Years ago you did enough.

"But how can I choose between your work
and mine?" Again, his voice, fine as dust:
Do the work that is most alive.
Some days it may be mine,
Most days it will be your own.
And finally you won't know the difference.

With one stroke I closed the seam.

—*Kim Stafford*

The Analyst Draws

Two days after your stroke, they hold out the crayon
you vigorously reject. Four days on

without language,
you do what you loved before language:

pick up a pencil and draw.
"Do you *know* how much raw

rejection you take?" you once asked me. Words
raked across my pink slips—words

you turned to after *your* rejection,
revealed at my therapy's end.
                                        Abstraction,

that's the method your studio teacher applied
when you were seventeen. Your father had just died.

The Radcliffe Dean had sent you
to learn the New Vision. But all you could do

was draw him dying. The Vision taught:
Drawing is Thought. *But what good were an oval and two dots,*

when they could have been his face and eyes?
Abstraction was just disguise,

so you took lines in an agony walk,
and after that class critique you'd walk

away from the studio—not to touch
a pencil for 30 years. Since touch

was exchanged for words,
you worked with what you overheard,

sensing beneath syllables their connecting lines.
How talented you became at drawing outlines

from the undisclosed shapes of inner life, teasing
out the pattern, taking

those lines for the walk to the interior
where I met you, wearier

when young than ever since. And ever since in awe
of the limning mind.
                          So draw,

as I was drawn to you,
                          as you drew me to you

till I could walk away,
                          as you now draw away.

—*Molly Peacock*

Early Morning Writing

—for William Stafford

Each time I nestle into your poems
I sense the quiet of my father's study,
the master bedroom of the house
saved for his ruminations.

His daughters had to knock
and ask for the tablets he let us use—
though not too many—the markers
he kept in a box, encouraging us to draw

fraktur. Shored up from his Amish boyhood,
the pooling quiet generated words
he thumped out on a Smith-Corona.
We could hear when he was working.

I sat down to write on the other side
of the closed door. Later, as a mother,
when I rose to write at four, I'd hear footsteps
on the stair and a child would appear

to curl up in the silence with me. Now,
from that morning seat, I sense the warmth
of those who snuggled in the place of poems.
The cat springs to the countertop, daring me to stay.

—Ann Hostetler

At the Stafford Birthday Celebration

His spirit flows,
eddies behind the last
row of orderly chairs, ripples

as introduced panelists disappear
behind stacks of qualifications.
The panel reveres

the poet's irreverence,
his urging students to find
their own voice. Audience comments

sought only in final moments,
we sense a whisper
in receding river voices—

>   *a life went by, just*
>   *a life, no claims…*

—*David Stallings*

This Morning I Want to Kick William Stafford in the Shins

To a successful, bustling, triumphant accomplisher: "What's your problem?"
        —William Stafford, *Daily Writings*

This morning I want to kick William Stafford in the shins.
It's after 9, and I'm still in my bathrobe. I willed the coffee weak.

Get going! Bill hollers from the carport again. *I've been up for seven
hours. I've been waiting to hear what you think of this line.* The night

before, I felt his owl-face hovering, his cool breath smelling
of pine. He paced and chanted, something about beauty and

diligence, something linking rivers, forgiveness, smoke.
I woke assuming I'd dreamt William Stafford in a sweater

vest in my bedroom. But on my breakfast plate: a fat manuscript
titled *Poems You'll Never Write on a Starry Almost-Morning*,

my typewriter scandalized, a note in its teeth. *"Do the hardest work
first,"* it taunts without error. *"Know the weight of a happy problem."*

I make him pack his bags for good. I tell him just how over it is, this
everyday submission—anyway, my friends are already famous. And I can

download whole seasons of *Masterpiece Theatre* to make me forget that
first stanza uncurling. I dash off to yoga, don't say good-bye, pretend

my core is a deep-roots kind of tree shunning to-do lists in *shavasana*.
I make my way home, after, up the steepest hill in town, nearly step on

a hummingbird flattened on the road, its body a silver piece of origami. Motion stopped. My life, all ears and arrows, leaning toward the right and easy words.

—Becca J.R. Lachman

Low Standards

Anybody could write if he would have standards as low as mine.
—William Stafford, *Writing the Australian Crawl*

A bite can last a lifetime
even if you don't know
what put its mouth on you
and tugged you toward who you are now.

It may have been a bite so light
you weren't sure it happened
but strong enough to pull you
down the line and through the water.

It may have resonated the upside down
question mark you baited yourself
like a string
pulling a tiny bell.

It may have been a strike—
that time you thought
you caught a shooting star
under all those waves.

A bite can last
a lifetime:
you can catch it
and never let go.

—William Palmer

The Muse of Work

If I could choose my muse,
she'd have red hair, short, spikey,
and green cateye glasses with rhinestones at the tips.
She'd wear a sleeveless dress, ruffled
over shallow scallop-shell breasts.
Can you see how young she is?
I think she's the girl Sappho loved,
the one with violets in her lap.
When she opens the door,
the white flurry of spring sweeps in.
But I've been assigned the Muse of Work,
a dead ringer for my mother
sipping black coffee, scrambling eggs,
a cigarette burning in a cut glass ash tray.
Then she opens the store. Amber whiskies
and clear vodkas shine on wooden shelves,
bruise-dark wine rising in the slender necks.
She fills in gaps where she's made a sale,
each pint and half-pint in its slot.
The phone's ringing, she's repeating,
Good morning Hy-Grade Liquors,
jotting down the order on a carboned pad.
What makes a thing beautiful?
She wears a dark jumper and a fresh blouse each day,
pats her armpits with talcum,
sweeps her lips with Cherries in the Snow.
She knows the pale sherry you crave,
sliding it into a brown paper bag, sized precisely.
There's the smell of newsprint and stale beer.
The cash register rings its tinny cymbal.
She steps out of the walk-in ice box
with a case of Pabst Blue Ribbon,

bumping the door closed with her hip.
There was something I needed, something
I wanted to ask her. But I had to wait.
Fifty years later, my mother dead,
when I search for the words to describe
a thing exactly—the smell of rain
or the sound a glass makes
when you set it down—I'm back there
standing in the corner of the store, watching her
as she takes the worn bills,
smoothes them in her palm.

—*Ellen Bass*

What You Missed That Day You Were Absent from Fourth Grade

Mrs. Nelson explained how to stand still and listen
to the wind, how to find meaning in pumping gas,

how peeling potatoes can be a form of prayer. She took
questions on how not to feel lost in the dark.

After lunch she distributed worksheets
that covered ways to remember your grandfather's

voice. Then the class discussed falling asleep
without feeling you had forgotten to do something else—

something important—and how to believe
the house you wake in is your home. This prompted

Mrs. Nelson to draw a chalkboard diagram detailing
how to chant the Psalms during cigarette breaks,

and how not to squirm for sound when your own thoughts
are all you hear; also, that you have enough.

The English lesson was that *I am*
is a complete sentence.

And just before the afternoon bell, she made the math equation
look easy. The one that proves that hundreds of questions,

and feeling cold, and all those nights spent looking
for whatever it was you lost, and one person

add up to something.

—*Brad Modlin*

Whenever I Get Home

Whenever I get home
after an exceptionally good day
in class, and I am smug
and full of myself, I am smug
and full of my own voice,
and I am still giddy
from how well it went,
from how articulate I was,
from how my one-liners zipped
along the rows around
the heads like hummingbirds,
I sit down in the uncomfortable
metal chair behind the house
in the shade of the trees,
close my eyes and remember
what William Stafford wrote,
Like a little stone, feel
the shadow of the great earth,
and the stupid grin wipes itself
off my stupid face, and then
wipes off my stupid face.

—*J.R. Solonche*

Report to William Stafford

Kansas, 2011

The poets were all
but defeated

They still wrote – still followed
the golden thread, as you said –
but only for themselves, it seemed

Which is all just
an artsy way of saying
We are now the only state in America without
an Arts Council and man it's embarrassing

*

If you were still around maybe you'd go
find the governor and read him
something full of kindness and light
that might change his mind and his life

*

Your art has had and will have better days

I bought your book at a Borders   I'm sorry to say
it had been there awhile   I could tell

though you I'm sure would not have
minded the dust

I found it on a back shelf

Other books had gathered around
as if to listen

—Jeff Tigchelaar

School Days

We invented language,
molded and rolled it
around the overheated room,
picking up ideas from every corner,
with light, traffic sounds and sirens

pouring in reminders of the plain
just outside, now decorated
red and green, with stars
and possibilities for giving and love.

I could be one. Each of you
another. Red and green.
Leaving for holiday, I pack
language and inventions we shaped, history
we made. Everyone's fingerprints are there.

—*Richard Levine*

After his death I talk about Bill Stafford's teaching methods

What did you learn? my husband asks.
I prop my head on my elbow so I can think better.
"Well, he taught me that a good teacher says just
about nothing! Did I tell you the story of how, in a restaurant
once, he heard some students in the next booth talking
about his class? One said, 'Did he ever say anything
about your poems?' The other said, 'I remember him saying
he thought I had a new typewriter ribbon!' And Bill just laughed..."
But how can a good teacher not say anything and teach?
He's drifting away; we haven't made love in months.
And I don't say a word.

—*Toi Derricotte*

On Buying a Deacquisitioned Book of William Stafford's Poetry Advertised on the Internet

When a poet dies, his books
are the last to hear it:
this one stood on the loading dock,
stoic, in its *lightly used* jacket,
in *good condition*,
wearing the rubber-stamped name
of its abandoner—
The Multnomah County Public Library.
Dismissed as an orphan, a vagrant,
the book lived a kind of half-life
in warehouses, ramshackle storefront
bookstores owned by men with thick glasses
or women in cat-hair cardigans
who like the smell of mildew and old paper
and the swamp light of failure.
It waited to be summoned,
to be loaded into a truck,
to travel the dark interstate
past fields and small towns the poet loved,
past distant farms,
barns haloed in yard-light.
It swam like a salmon
up an ever-narrowing source,
and landed on a front porch,
swaddled in bubble wrap.
Freed at last, and brought in
under the circle of a reading lamp,
it fell readily open,
displayed its *minimal markings*—

a small grease spot in the margin,
a faint pencil line
beneath a word—
which let you know
others had held it once
in open palms,
and drank from its quiet sounds.

—*James Armstrong*

The Ocean Effect

In this blue-shuttered season of winter,
I have fallen in with silence.
My cat leans into me, trembles a bit,
rests her head on my foot.
On the kitchen table,
a vase hugs the remains of a tulip.
Its dropped purple petals
resemble quiet tongues. I make little piles,
and think of my students.

A young girl crosses the street
in the evening darkness. *She appeared
out of nowhere,* the driver said – *like a ghost.*
The empty desk sobers us. After
school, I rearrange the seating.

This morning, I sip dark coffee,
watch thick flakes fall in a hurry,
rush the ground where they
amount to nothing.

—*Mary Ellen Redmond*

A Hesitant Love Poem to Second Period English on the Occasion of Valentine's Day

—after themes in William Stafford's "Lit Instructor"

Now listen up, class.
This is hard to say.

See, I remember the shock
of spotting Miss Duryee
pushing her cart at the market
past the oranges, mounded high,
and her saying hello
and chatting calmly with my mother
as I stared dumbfounded
at my first grade teacher
out in the world.

Now I loved Miss Duryee
and learning to read at her orderly tables,
coloring within careful boundaries,
finding out what a paragraph was
and how vowels said their letter names
but had secret sounds, too,
and how to carefully line up sums.

But this sighting in the market
did not line up.
Why was she *there*?

Miss Duryee had her world,
where Bluebirds sat at one table
and Robins at another,
where paste and paint
had their own cubbyholes,
where paragraphs were clearly indented.

The store was not her place,
but full of disorder:
potatoes dumped drunkenly in bins,
grapes squashed on the linoleum floor,
that pile-up of oranges,
and people in crooked check-out lines
like my mom and me.
I loved Miss Duryee,
but love has its careful boundaries.

So it's hard for me to figure out
how to tell you, class,
what I feel for you this day.
Things have their secret sounds, their place.

A bluebird squawks
outside the classroom window.

Those oranges were bright
and stacked to the sky.

—*Tim Gillespie*

Talking to Stafford Late at Night

Never mind that you're a morning person, or 18 years dead—
I hear you over my left shoulder. "Maybe," you say,
then nod. Outside, the pink sky has dissolved to black.
The snow exhales. Temperatures drop. The waning moon climbs
over the cusp of exhausted cedars. Juncos, chickadees and occasional
branches of sadness sleep. "Maybe what?" I ask,
keeping my hand moving on the window of the page.

Outside, you see what you always saw: dark on dark,
a glimmer of movement, a low call from where
the air glitters into itself. Behind the curtain of winter, spring.
Inside spring, lilac, hard to imagine. Yet the dirt
still manages to inhale the sky and make itself porous.
We wait together for me to find what I'm looking for.
Not something known and lost but the opposite. My hands
breathe. The steady almost undetectable buzz of everything
sings toward the wide arms of the dark horizon.

World, I could say if I were you, or Friend,
what would you have me do so that the perfect music
could come out, juxtaposing dark and home, song and field,
abandoned house of the heart and noiseless crowd of tall grass?
You wait in the dark, showing me time itself turns on "maybe,"
the "no" of what we cannot bear, the "yes" of all that is.

—*Caryn Mirriam-Goldberg*

Stafford's Body

The house that held him
now a box of wind

between its boards the light
slides in both directions

and critters we can't name
call it home

weather moves it
it's weather through and through

its stairs
sing back with every step

—Wyatt Townley

Ars Poetica

—after William Stafford

To become unreachable
in the far corners of rural darkness
where the soft-tilled edges of civilized
    fields meld to the wild.

Children who ran too far would be lost,
        evaporating into story book
endings—caught in bear traps, eaten
by coyotes or taken and raised
    for their own.
     .

Their games but filaments, spiders
letting their webs to the dark,
    tenuous tethers of the known world.

Rope slacked and rope pulled,
    Night was just beginning
        to extinguish them.

They will pick up again tomorrow,
    in these wind-swept fields
        where art begins.

—Sarah Estes

IV.

June 23, 1953 draft of "A Ritual to Read To Each Other"
(reduced)
by William Stafford.

Study Guide

The editor hopes readers will keep William Stafford's books nearby, and that often two or more books can be opened in poetic conversation. Readers may find Stafford's *The Way It Is: New & Selected Poems* (1998) and *Ask Me: 100 Poems* (2014)—both from Graywolf Press—especially helpful.

Section I

1. Paulann Petersen's poem "From the Very Start" reveals that William Stafford's first word was *moon*. Write a poem about the first word *you* uttered; or the first word you *wish* you had spoken; or the first word that surfaces when you think of William Stafford.

2. David Lee's poem is called "Big Bend Triptych." Make up your own definition of *triptych* and write a poem that follows your invented guidelines and describes a place you've explored. Next, look up what a triptych poem really is and write one of your own (See David Lee's bio for more information about his poem's inspiration.)

3. Several contributions in this anthology utilize short excerpts from William Stafford's poetry. What lines from Stafford's poems have stayed with you, and why? Try writing a poem that uses one of them as a springboard.

4. *Apostrophe* is one figure of speech used in Philip Dacey's poem "Telling William Stafford's Ghost Why I Moved to New York City." Look up the definition of this term, then experiment with using apostrophe in a poem that puts William Stafford in a setting readers wouldn't expect to find him.

5. After reading Joel Peckham's "The Noise We Make" and William Stafford's "Assurances" (p. 153, *The Way It Is*), find a public spot, sit alone, and devote 20 minutes to mindfully paying attention to

the world around you. "Freewrite" what your five senses experience (without censoring or revising your writing). After the 20 minutes, study what you wrote. Circle any lines that could jumpstart a poem.

6. Experiment with writing a stanza that uses only one word per line, in the spirit of Jesse Nathan's poem, "What Do You Really Believe."

7. Meg Hutchinson uses a line from William Stafford's poem "You Reading This, Be Ready" as an epigraph. Read this Stafford poem aloud (p. 45, *The Way It Is*) then let the line Meg chose as her epigraph become a writing prompt for your own answer.

8. Write your own *renga* (either with another writer or using excerpts from a poem) after looking up its definition and using Mary Rose O'Reilley's poem "Renga" as a springboard.

9. Some of Stafford's most well-known poems speak of seeing the world as a child or parent. Paul Merchant's poem is titled "Instructions for Childhood." Write your own poem using this same title—or, write a poem based on the instructions you think William Stafford might give.

10. On your next hike, keep David Shumate's poem "Bringing Things Back from the Woods" in mind. Keep track of what grabs your attention; when you're home, write a list poem of highlights. Or, write a poem that deviates from David's title by changing "Woods" to a place you visit (or wish you visited) often.

11. Several poems in this anthology are in dialogue with William Stafford's "Traveling through the Dark." With this poem handy (p. 77, *The Way It Is),* or after listening to Stafford read it aloud, discuss which anthology poems connect to this poem, and why. (http://www.williamstaffordarchives.org/browse/audio/)

12. Read William Stafford's poem "Our Cave" (p. 189, *The Way It Is*) alongside the anthology poem "Daoist Out of Kansas" by Charles Goodrich. Write a poem describing one of your childhood hiding spots.

13. Jaswinder Bolina's "The Last National" is partially inspired by Stafford's three-line poem, "Indian Caves in the Dry Country" (see

whole poem below, and on p. 47, *The Darkness Around Us is Deep*). After reading Stafford's poem below, write a list of the first ten things that come to mind—is there energy in this list for a poem of your own?

"Indian Caves in the Dry Country"

There are some canyons
we might use again
sometime.

14. After reading "The Poet's Hand" by Terry Blythe, reflect on Stafford's "Ceremony" (p. 61, *The Way It Is*). Stafford often wrote about Oregon and Kansas. What places do you highlight or seek in your own poems and reading life? What places do you avoid? Why?

15. Hearing Todd Davis read his poem at a writing conference sparked the idea for this anthology. Have you ever had a dream with William Stafford in it? If so, write about it in poem form. Or, experiment with keeping a dream journal for a week. Before you get out of bed in the morning, write down any dreams you remember; come back to them for poem ideas.

16. Read William Stafford's "On a Church Lawn" (p. 5, *The Way It Is*) alongside Mark Thalman's "Church." What other Stafford poems could enter into this conversation?

17. William Stafford sometimes used humor in his poems about very serious subjects. Locate a few of these, then discuss anthology poems that nod to his expertise use of a satirical or sardonic tone.

18. Ken McCullough was drawn to William Stafford's poem "Everything Twice" (p. 4, *My Name is William Tell*) because it seemed so unlike most of Stafford's other work, "maybe even an exercise").[1] As a writing exercise of your own, choose a poem by William Stafford and pen its parody.

19. Many contributors in this anthology knew or met William

---

1 Personal correspondence

Stafford before his death in 1993. If you were also lucky enough to be in this category, write a poem of your own detailing a memorable meeting with Stafford. Or, write a poem in which you meet William Stafford in a dream or unexpected place.

Section II

1. "Happiness" by Ingrid Wendt takes its inspiration from Stafford's poem "Why I Am Happy" (p. 20, *The Way It Is*). Study the poems side-by-side and discuss the conversations between them. Why do you think Wendt's poem appears in this section of the anthology?

2. After reading Stafford's "News Every Day" (p. 34, *The Way It Is*), shape a poem with the same title as Chloe Honum's contribution, "Evening News." Perhaps experiment with making William Stafford the poem's speaker.

3. Paul Fericano's "Thirty-Two" imagines the alternative point of view of a minor character in Stafford's poem "Fifteen" (p. 9, *The Rescued Year*). Read these poems in answer to one another, then choose a character from another Stafford poem. Create a persona poem about this person's possible point of view.

4. Use the online source http://civilianpublicservice.org/ to research two of the WWII conscientious objector work camps highlighted in this anthology, Los Prietos and Cascade Locks. What kinds of work, projects, and discoveries came out of "CPS"?

5. Though he had relatives and friends who served in the military, William Stafford chose to join Civilian Public Service when he was drafted. Write a poem about someone you know with military experience, or who has completed alternative service of some kind.

6. How is Margaret Chula's poem "Equilibrium" in dialogue with other themes and voices in this section? What was "Topaz, the Jewel of the Desert"?

7. Thomas R. Smith had Stafford's poem "Peace Walk" (p. 9, *The Way It Is*) in mind when he wrote his poem "Peace Vigil." How do these two poems connect with—and push against—each other?

8. There are echoes of William Stafford's poem "At the Bomb Testing Site" (p. 67, *The Way It Is*) in Derek Sheffield's "Breathing in Wartime." What would you add to the conversation between these two poems?

9. "Things I Learned at Sixty-Six" by Patricia Wixon is a list poem in couplets. It also uses Stafford's "Things I Learned Last Week" (p. 195, *The Way It Is*) as its springboard. Freewrite ideas for your own list poem, exploring things you have learned or wish you had by a certain age.

10. According to Connie Wanek, her poem "Catbird" "echos Stafford's conviction that the modest tragedies of the natural world provide us with a glimpse into our own fragility, and paradoxically give us courage."[2] Make a list of "modest tragedies" you have witnessed in the natural world, then use one idea to start a new poem.

11. Animals often appear in the poetry of William Stafford. Looking through the titles of *The Way It Is: New & Selected Poems* or *Ask Me: 100 Poems* (Graywolf Press), make a list of the animals he uses most often, then read and discuss some of these poems. How are the poems that use animals in this anthology "in conversation" with Stafford's animal poems? What animals appear in your own poems? Write a poem with an animal you've never featured before.

12. William Stafford is known for having written every day and early in the morning. What poems in this anthology speak to this routine? What's your own writing process? What time of day do you usually write, and why? Share your writing habits in a writing group.

13. After reading Kathleen Gunton's poem, look up the definition of *cento* and use the poems in this anthology to create one of your own.

2 Personal correspondence

Section III

1. If you're a writer, what writing advice have you received that's steered you—on or off course? Write a poem that uses such advice as a first line or epigraph.

2. Read Stafford's poem "The Way I Write" (p. 32-3, *The Way It Is*) alongside Peter Quinn's "Compliments and Complaints." How would you describe your own body language when you read or write poetry? Let this be a start to a poem.

3. Read David Citino's poem "Charms Against Writer's Block," then write a poem of your own using— or playing with—its title.

4. Molly Peacock reflects on her poem: "I met William Stafford only once, in the early 1970s, after he gave a remarkable reading of his poems in Binghamton, NY, hosted by the poet Milton Kessler. Then in my twenties, I sat moping on the stairwell at Kessler's party. Stafford had to get past me to go upstairs, and as I raised my head toward him, he beamed at me an uplifting smile. Ever since, I've connected him with uplift. At the time I was trying to separate the strands of creativity and craziness. The prevailing myth was that a poet needed her neuroses, no matter how destructive, and that a therapist's drive toward ordinary thinking would so normalize you that you wouldn't be a poet anymore. Not long after that party I decided that there had to be sanity in art making, and that, in fact, art making was the sanest part of my life, something that William Stafford understood profoundly. It is part of the source of his practice as a poet, the basis of his commitment to the daily making of art.

    A few blocks away from the house where Stafford beamed the beneficent smile stood the office of the psychotherapist in this poem. She deeply understood the creative process, and with her I began a long journey, maintaining contact for thirty-eight years now.

    After her stroke, I watched her meet the challenge of reconstructing her life—through art. As she began drawing (and later painting) every day, I witnessed again the uplift of the daily repetitive custom William Stafford advocated. *The smile of the pencil*, if you will. While in style my poem "The Analyst Draws" is not something I think Stafford would have gravitated toward (he wasn't a rhyming couplets kind of guy), the intent, to me, feels very much a part of his gentle insistence on the profundity of an artist's daily routine."[3]

5. The Friends of William Stafford plan and promote Stafford birthday readings every year, partly to celebrate William Stafford's legacy (See http://williamstafford.org/pages/events.html for a list of annual events.) The anthology poem by David Stallings recalls such an event and highlights an excerpt from William Stafford's poem "Vita" (p. 52, *The Way It Is*). Write a poem for the 100th anniversary of William's Stafford's birth—and consider reading it at a local Stafford centennial celebration in 2014.

6. Stafford's "When I Met My Muse" (p. 22, *The Way It Is*) inspired Ellen Bass to write a poem about her own muse ("The Muse of Work"). Read these two poems in dialogue with each other, then write your own muse poem.

7. "What You Missed That Day You Were Absent from Fourth Grade" echoes the spirit of Brad Modlin's favorite William Stafford poem "A Story That Could Be True" (p. 49, *The Way It Is*). Write a poem or letter in response to what you'd consider your favorite William Stafford poem—or the Stafford poem that follows you around, for whatever reason.

Section IV

Study the hand-written draft of "A Ritual to Read to Each Other" included in this anthology. Compare it to the final printed version (p. 75, *The Way It Is*) and to the versions featured online at the William Stafford Archives (http://williamstaffordarchives.org/browse/poems/).

3 Personal correspondence

Notes on Contributors

James Armstrong is the author of two books, *Monument in a Summer Hat* (New Issues Press, 1999) and *Blue Lash* (Milkweed Editions, 2006). He came late to Stafford's work but now has a signed typescript of "Traveling through the Dark" hanging above his writing desk. He is a Professor of English at Winona State University in Winona, Minnesota, where he lives with his family. **(p. 144)**

Tim Barnes taught for twenty-five years in the English Department at Portland Community College. His latest book of poems is *Definitions for a Lost Language*. He co-edited *Wood Works: The Life and Writings of Charles Erskine Scott Wood* and now edits *The Friends of William Stafford Newsletter*. He first met Bill in the mid seventies when he was in graduate school at Portland State University. **(p. 40)**

Poetry books by **Ellen Bass** include *The Human Line* and *Mules of Love*, and she has a new collection, *Like A Beggar,* forthcoming from Copper Canyon Press in early 2014. Her poems have recently been published in *The New Yorker, American Poetry Review*, and *Ploughshares*. Ellen teaches in the MFA poetry program at Pacific University. **(p. 135)**

Claire Bateman's books are *Locals, The Bicycle Slow Race, Friction, At the Funeral of the Ether, Clumsy, Leap,* and *Coronology*. She has been awarded Individual Artist Fellowships from the NEA, the Tennessee Arts Commission, and the Surdna Foundation, as well as two Pushcart Prizes. She is poetry editor of the *St. Katherine Review*. **(p. 111)**

Marvin Bell and William Stafford wrote two books back and forth: *Segues: A Conversation in Poetry* (Godine, 1983) and *Annie-Over* (Honeybrook Press, 1988), the latter written in July, 1984, while both were teaching for the Centrum Writers' Conference in Port Townsend, and from which Bell's poem in this collection is taken. · Bell's latest book is *Vertigo: The Living Dead Man Poems*. **(p. 26)**

Robert Bly's new selected poems, *Stealing Sugar from the Castle*, was published this fall by W. W. Norton, and Graywolf Press recently published *Airmail: The Letters of Robert Bly and Tomas Tranströmer*. He lives with his wife Ruth in Minneapolis. **(p. 19)**

Terry Blythe lives in rural Kansas where she earns a living as a rancher and as an English teacher. Her poems have appeared in *5 A.M.*, *Any Key Review*, *The Kenyon Review*, and a book review in *Prairie Schooner*, all under her former name, Ms. Terry Cox. She is a graduate of the Bennington MFA Writing Program. **(p. 37)**

Jaswinder Bolina is the author of *Phantom Camera*, winner of the 2012 Green Rose Prize in Poetry from New Issues Press and *Carrier Wave*, winner of the 2006 Colorado Prize for Poetry. *Phantom Camera* is available from New Issues in the U.S. and from Hachette India internationally. He is currently on the MFA faculty at the University of Miami. **(p. 36)**

Emily K. Bright holds an MFA in poetry from the University of Minnesota. Her chapbook *Glances Back* was published by Pudding House Press, and her individual poems have appeared in such literary journals and anthologies as *Other Voices International, North American Review, The Pedestal Magazine,* and *Come Together: Imagine Peace.* Follow her commentary on writing and social justice at http://emilykbright.blogspot.com. **(p. 102)**

Early in his life, **Paul Brooke** read and relished William Stafford's work. Brooke returns to those books each year. Today, Brooke is the author of *Light and Matter* and *Mediations on Egrets.* These combine photography and poetry together in symbiotic ways. He is professor of English at Grand View University, where he teaches contemporary literature, creative writing, and literary theory. **(p. 93)**

Robert Cantoni studied creative writing in Athens, Ohio. His work has previously appeared in *Michigan Quarterly Review, Timothy McSweeney's Internet Tendency,* and in other publications. He lives in Cleveland, Ohio, where he makes apps for the iPhone and iPad with Nice Mohawk Limited, a company he co-founded. **(p. 90)**

Margaret Chula has published six poetry collections, including *What Remains: Japanese Americans in Internment Camps* with quilt artist Cathy Erickson. Recent poems have appeared in *Prairie Schooner, Kyoto Journal, Poet Lore, Briarcliff Review, Windfall, Sufi Journal,* and *West Marin Review.* Maggie serves as president of the Tanka Society of America and as poet laureate for Friends of Chamber Music. **(p. 84)**

Born in Cleveland, Ohio, **David Citino** (1947-2005) published a dozen poetry books during his lifetime and taught for over thirty years at Ohio State, where he was also named poet laureate of the school. His many awards included fellowships from the National Endowment for the Arts and the Ohio Arts Council, and the Ohioana Career Award from the Ohioana Library Association. (**p. 124**)

Philip Dacey, winner of three Pushcart Prizes, has published eleven books, including *Mosquito Operas: New and Selected Short Poems* (Rain Mountain Press, 2010), *Vertebrae Rosaries: 50 Sonnets* (Red Dragonfly Press, 2008), and whole collections about Gerard Manley Hopkins, Thomas Eakins, and New York City. His forthcoming twelfth book, *Gimme Five*, won the Blue Light Press 2012 Book Award. (**p. 27**)

Jim Daniels is the author of fourteen books of poetry, including *Birth Marks* (BOA, 2013). He has received the Brittingham Prize for Poetry, the Tillie Olsen Prize, the Blue Lynx Poetry Prize, two fellowships from the National Endowment for the Arts, and two from the Pennsylvania Council on the Arts. His poems have appeared in the Pushcart Prize and Best American Poetry anthologies. At Carnegie Mellon University, he is the Thomas Stockham Professor of English. (**p. 92**)

Betty Davis retired from the Norfolk Police Department after twenty-eight years of service. She also served in the United States Army Reserve. Previous work published in *Rattle*. Betty Davis resides in Norfolk, Virginia. (**p. 80**)

Todd Davis teaches creative writing and environmental studies at Penn State University's Altoona College. His four poetry books include *In the Kingdom of the Ditch* and *The Least of These*. He also edited *Fast Break to Line Break: Poets on the Art of Basketball* and co-edited *Making Poems: Forty Poems with Commentary by the Poets*. His work has appeared in such places as *The American Poetry Review, Poetry Daily, Gettysburg Review, Shenandoah, North American Review*, and *Iowa Review*. (**p. 39**)

Toi Derricotte is the author of five books of poetry, most recently *The Undertaker's Daughter* (2011). Her literary memoir, *The Black Notebooks*, won the 1998 Anisfield-Wolf Book Award for Non-Fiction and was a *New York Times* Notable Book of the Year. Her honors include fellowships from the National Endowment for the Arts and the Guggenheim Foundation. With Cornelius Eady, she co-founded Cave Canem Foundation, North America's premier "home for black poetry." **(p. 143)**

When not writing poetry, **James Dickson** teaches English and Creative Writing at Germantown High School, just outside of Jackson, Mississippi. An MFA graduate from the Bennington Writing Seminars, he lives with his wife, Greer, and their son. Some of his poems appear in *Ruminate, Hospital Drive, The Louisiana Review, Spillway, Amoskeag, Slant, The Fiddleback,* and *Two Hawks Quarterly.* **(p. 76)**

George Drew was born in Mississippi and now lives in upstate New York. He is the author of five volumes, most recently *The View from Jackass Hill*, winner of the 2010 X.J. Kennedy Poetry Prize from Texas Review Press. George has published widely, most recently in *Bloodroot, Naugatuck River Review* and *The Texas Review.* **(p. 104)**

Sarah Estes' work has appeared in *Agni, Cimmaron Review, Crab Orchard Review, Field, New Orleans Review, Southern Review* and elsewhere. She is the author of *Hive Bone* (Finishing Line Press) and has been a Hoynes Fellow at the University of Virginia. **(p. 151)**

Dennis Etzel Jr. lives in Topeka, Kansas. He has an MFA from The University of Kansas and an MA and Certificate in Women and Gender Studies from Kansas State. His work has appeared in *Denver Quarterly, Indiana Review, Blaze, VOX, Fact-Simile, 1913: a journal of poetic forms, 3:AM, DIAGRAM,* and elsewhere. He teaches English at Washburn University, is Managing Editor for Woodley Press and a TALK Scholar for the Kansas Humanities Council, and volunteers at YWCA's Center for Safety and Empowerment. **(p. 119)**

Paul Fericano is a poet and satirist and co-founder of the parody news syndicate, *Yossarian Universal News Service.* He is the author of several books of poetry, including *Commercial Break, Cancer Quiz,* and *Loading the Revolver with Real Bullets.* In the forthcoming year

The New Yorker, The Atlantic Monthly, and *The Paris Review* are all expected to reject his work. **(p. 74)**

Helen Frost's books include seven novels-in-poems for children and teens, two collections of poetry for adults, two plays, a book about teaching young people to write about difficult issues, three picture books for younger readers, and two anthologies. She has worked extensively with children and teens, helping them to live nonviolently. She lives in Fort Wayne, Indiana. **(p. 99)**

Trina Gaynon is a graduate of the MFA program in Creative Writing at University of San Francisco. Her poems have appeared in the anthologies *Bombshells* and *Knocking at the Door*, as well as numerous journals including *Natural Bridge, Reed* and the final issue of *Runes*. **(p. 34)**

Dan Gerber's eighth collection of poems, *Sailing through Cassiopeia* (Copper Canyon Press, 2012) received the 2013 Midland Authors Book Award for Poetry. Also the author of three novels, a book of short stories and two nonfiction books, his work has appeared in *Poetry, Narrative, The New Yorker, Massachusetts Review*, and *Best American Poetry*. **(p. 61)**

Tim Gillespie taught public high school English in Oregon for almost four decades. For many years he also co-directed the summer Oregon Writing Project at Lewis & Clark College with Kim Stafford. His latest book, *Doing Literary Criticism*, was recently published by Stenhouse. His poems have appeared in *Cloudbank, Sequoia, Northwest Magazine, English Journal*, and other places. **(p. 147)**

Charles Goodrich's books include *Insects of South Corvallis, Going to Seed: Dispatches from the Garden, The Practice of Home,* and *A Scripture of Crows*. Following a long career as a professional gardener, he presently serves as Director for the Spring Creek Project for Ideas, Nature, and the Written Word at Oregon State University. **(p. 35)**

Craig Goodworth is an interdisciplinary artist working in drawing, installation, poetry, and prose. Core themes in his art are the body and place. Holding master's degrees in sustainable communities and fine art, he has received fellowships in art and writing and has served as an artist-in-residence in various contexts. Craig, his wife, and son reside in Oregon. **(p. 67)**

Jeff Gundy's latest books, his ninth and tenth, are *Songs from an Empty Cage: Poetry, Mystery, Anabaptism, and Peace* (poetics, Cascadia, 2013), and *Somewhere Near Defiance* (poems, Anhinga, 2014). Recent work is in *The Sun, The Georgia Review, Kenyon Review, Nimrod*, and *Image*. A 2008 Fulbright Lecturer at the University of Salzburg, he teaches at Bluffton University in Ohio. **(p. 75)**

Kathleen Gunton is working on a collection of cento poems where "voices whisper in..." as William Stafford once wrote. Her poems and photography often appear in the same journals; she believes one art feeds another. Recent work appears in *Arts & Letters, Switchback, Thema, Healing Muse, Off The Coast*, and the anthology *Monkscript Two: Surprising Saints*. **(p. 108)**

Patrick Hicks has published five poetry collections, most recently *Finding the Gossamer* and *This London*. The Bush Artist Foundation and the National Endowment for the Humanities have both recognized his work. He is Writer-in-Residence at Augustana College and, during the summer months, you'll usually find him in Ireland. His first novel, *The Commandant of Lubizec*, is forthcoming from Steerforth Press. **(p. 64)**

Chloe Honum's poems have appeared in *The Paris Review, Poetry, The Southern Review, Best New Poets*, and elsewhere. She is a recipient of a Ruth Lilly Fellowship from the Poetry Foundation. **(p. 72)**

Ann Hostetler is the author of a volume of poetry, *Empty Room with Light,* and editor of *A Cappella: Mennonite Voices in Poetry* (Iowa, 2003). Her poems have appeared in numerous journals and anthologies. She teaches at Goshen College in Goshen, Indiana and is co-editor of the *Journal of the Center for Mennonite Writing* at www.mennonitewriting.org. **(p. 130)**

Joan Houlihan is the author of four books of poetry: *The Us, The Mending Worm*, winner of the Green Rose Award, *Hand-Held*

Executions: Poems & Essays, and *Ay*. She is also author of *Boston Comment*, a series of critical essays. She founded and directs the Colrain Poetry Manuscript Conference and Concord Poetry Center, and teaches at Clark University and in Lesley University's Low-Residency MFA Program. **(p. 86)**

Jan Hutchinson has been writing and studying poetry for over fifty years. Inspired by William Stafford's pre-dawn devotion to his art, Jan has written at least one poem each morning for a decade. She has published and given readings only locally, but, in the life she's lived, poetry has been the center pole that has held up the whole circus. **(p. 51)**

Meg Hutchinson grew up in the Berkshires of Western Massachusetts. She is an award-winning songwriter and recording artist on Red House Records and tours widely in North America and Europe. She is also a mental health advocate and speaks about recovery at conferences, schools and hospitals. She lives in Boston. **(p. 30)**

Joseph Hutchison is the author of 14 collections of poems, most recently *Thread of the Real* and *The Earth-Boat* (both released in 2012). He makes his living as a writer and teacher of graduate writing and literature courses at the University of Denver's University College. He lives with his wife Melody Madonna in the foothills southwest of Denver. **(p. 20)**

The poems of **D.R. James** have appeared in various magazines, three chapbooks (from Finishing Line Press and Pudding House), and the full-length collection *Since Everything Is All I've Got* (March Street Press). He lives in Holland, Michigan, where he has taught writing and literature at Hope College for 28 years, and where William Stafford visited in the 1980s. **(p. 79)**

Paul Keller's poetry has appeared in: *Wilderness, Appalachia, Chicago Review, Jeopardy*, and *Fireweed*. A fourth-generation Oregonian with a BS in journalism from the University of Oregon, he abandoned the newsroom to launch a new career as wilderness ranger and hotshot firefighter with the U.S. Forest Service. He is the writer-editor for the national Wildland Fire Lessons Learned Center. **(p. 52)**

Stuart Kestenbaum is the author of three books of poems, most recently *Prayers and Run-on Sentences* (Deerbrook Editions 2007) and a collection of essays about craft, community and creativity, *The View from Here* (Brynmorgen Press, 2012). He lives in Deer Isle, Maine, where he is the director of the Haystack Mountain School of Crafts. **(p. 106)**

Greg Kimura lives and writes in Palo Alto, California. His book of poetry *Cargo* can be purchased at http://gregkimura.com. **(p. 54)**

Maxine Hong Kingston is author of *The Woman Warrior: Memoirs of a Girlhood Among Ghosts, China Men, Tripmaster Monkey – His Fake Book, Hawai'I One Summer, To Be the Poet, The Fifth Book of Peace,* and *I Love a Broad Margin to My Life.* **(p. 94)**

Susan Kinsolving's books of poems are *The White Eyelash, Dailies & Rushes,* a finalist for The National Book Critics Circle Award, and *Among Flowers.* Forthcoming is her new collection, *My Glass Eye.* She has taught in The Bennington Writing Seminars, University of Connecticut, Southampton College, Chautauqua Institute, Willard-Cybulski Men's Prison, California Institute of the Arts, and The Hotchkiss School. **(p. 22)**

Ted Kooser was privileged to have Bill Stafford take his photograph in Brookings, SD, in the early 1970s, and used that picture on the back of one of his early books. For some mysterious reason he looks forty years younger in that photo than he does today. **(p. 41)**

Becca J.R. Lachman teaches and tutors at Ohio University in Athens, Ohio. *The Apple Speaks,* her first book of poems, is dedicated "to humanitarian workers around the globe, but more for the families who love them" (Cascadia, 2012). **(p. 132)**

David Lee, retired, splits his time between Bandera, Texas and Seaside, Oregon, where he scribbles and wanders available trails and byways, all at about the same rate and pace. He is in intensive training to achieve his goal of becoming a world-class piddler. "Big Bend Triptych" was written after several days of wandering in the Tejas desert when a visit to Terlingua and then Santa Elena Canyon and the clear Rio Grande river whispering "ask me" brought forth memories of Bill Stafford and times spent with him in the Utah desert long ago. **(p. 23)**

Richard Levine is the author of *That Country's Soul, A Language Full of Wars and Songs, Snapshots from a Battle*, and *A Tide of a Hundred Mountains*. "Bread," a poem from his newest book, is featured in Ted Kooser's *American Life in Poetry* column. You can find his "Talkin' Frackin' Blues," on YouTube. A retired teacher, he is learning to steward an agro-forest. **(p. 142)**

Perie Longo has published three books of poetry: *Milking The Earth, The Privacy of Wind,* and *With Nothing Behind But Sky: a journey through grief,* as well as having poems published in several journals and anthologies. Her fourth volume, *Baggage Claim,* is slated for publication by WordTech Editions in January, 2014. She was Poet Laureate of Santa Barbara from 2007-09. **(p. 113)**

Denise Low, second Kansas Poet Laureate, has 20 books of poetry and essays, including *Ghost Stories* (best Native American Books of 2010, *The Circle;* Kansas Notable Book). She edited *Kansas Poems of William Stafford* (Woodley). Her poetry appears in *New Letters, North American Review, Yellow Medicine Review, American Life in Poetry,* and *Summerset Review.* She is a 2008-2013 board member of AWP. **(p. 49)**

Christina Lux's poetry has appeared on NPR and in *Women's Studies Quarterly, The Delmarva Review, To the Stars through Difficulty, Salome Magazine,* and *27 rue de fleures.* She is Assistant Director of the Center for the Humanities at UC Merced. https://twitter.com/ca_lux. **(p. 87)**

Teresa McNeil MacLean, Santa Ynez, CA poet, artist, guitarist-singer-songwriter, has written natural free verse for forty years. She teaches, since 1986, poetry workshops for children, includes poetry in her art exhibits, and posts her daily haiku on *Facebook* during National Poetry Month each year, sharing her poetry way of seeing the world. **(p. 55)**

Mary Makofske's book *Traction* (Ashland Poetry Press, 2011) won the Richard Snyder Award. Her poems have appeared in *Poetry,*

Mississippi Review, Natural Bridge, Poetry East, Louisville Review, Asheville Poetry Review, and other journals and anthologies. She is also the author of *The Disappearance of Gargoyles* and *Eating Nasturtiums*, winner of a Flume Press Chapbook Award. **(p. 77)**

Fred Marchant is the author of four books of poetry, including *The Looking House* (Graywolf Press, 2009). His first book, *Tipping Point,* winner of the 1993 Word Works Washington Prize, has been re-issued in a twentieth anniversary second edition. Founding director of the Poetry Center at Suffolk University in Boston, he is also the editor of *Another World Instead: The Early Poems of William Stafford, 1937-1947* (Graywolf Press, 2008). **(p. 63)**

Quitman Marshall was born and raised in Columbia, SC, moved to Barcelona, then D.C., Amherst, and NYC. He was the founding coordinator of the Literary Series at Spoleto Festival USA. His chapbooks include *The Birth Gift*, *14th Street*, and *The Slow Comet*. In 1996 he won the Writers Exchange Award sponsored by Poets & Writers, Inc. He moved to Paris in 1999, and since 2001 has lived in Beaufort, SC, with his wife, Martine, and their three children. **(p. 69)**

Ken McCullough lives in Winona, MN and is a former Poet Laureate of Winona. His most recent and seventh book of poetry is *Broken Gates* (Red Dragonfly Press). He has worked closely with Cambodian poet U Sam Oeur on U's poetry, *Sacred Vows* (a bilingual edition), as well as U's memoir, *Crossing Three Wildernesses*, both with Coffee House Press. **(p. 48)**

Wendy McVicker is a Teaching Artist and Literature Field Consultant for the Ohio Arts Council's Arts Learning program. Her poetry has appeared in small journals online and in print, and in the anthology *Red Thread, Gold Thread: The Poet's Voice*. She performs her poetry with musician Emily Prince as the duo *another language altogether.* **(p. 114)**

Ed Meek has had poetry, fiction and articles in *The Sun, The Paris Review, Cream City Review, North American Review*, etc. He teaches creative writing and composition at Austin Prep School and lives with his wife in Somerville, MA. **(p. 115)**

A native of Wales, **Paul Merchant** taught at Warwick University before spending sixteen years as Director of the William Stafford Archives in Portland, Oregon. He co-edited two volumes of William Stafford's prose: *Crossing Unmarked Snow* (1998) and *The Answers Are Inside the Mountains* (2003). His fourth poetry collection *Some Business of Affinity* was a 2007 Oregon Book Awards finalist, and his translations of modern Greek poet Yannis Ritsos include *Monochords* (2008) and *Twelve Poems about Cavafy* (2010). **(p. 32)**

Philip Metres is the author of *A Concordance of Leaves* (2013), *abu ghraib arias* (2011), *To See the Earth* (2008), and *Behind the Lines: War Resistance Poetry on the American Homefront since 1941* (2007). His work has garnered NEA fellowships, four Ohio Arts Council Grants, the Arab American Book Award, and the Cleveland Arts Prize. He teaches at John Carroll University. **(p. 82)**

Bryce Milligan has been the publisher, editor, and designer for Wings Press since 1995. Throughout the 1980s and '90s he edited various pacifist and multicultural literary journals and anthologies. He is the author of several award-winning children's and young adult books, as well as six collections of poetry, his latest being *Lost and Certain of It* (London: Aark Arts, 2006). **(p. 43)**

Caryn Mirriam-Goldberg, the 2009-2013 Poet Laureate of Kansas, is author of sixteen books, including a novel, *The Divorce Girl*; a non-fiction book, *Needle in the Bone: How a Holocaust Survivor & Polish Resistance Fighter Beat the Odds and Found Each Other*, and four poetry collections. Founder of Transformative Language Arts at Goddard College where she teaches, Mirriam-Goldberg leads writing workshops widely. **(p. 149)**

Brad Modlin's poetry, fiction, and creative nonfiction have appeared—or are forthcoming—in *Denver Quarterly, Indiana Review, The Florida Review, Rhino, River Teeth,* and others. He is a PhD candidate in creative writing at Ohio University, where he reads for *New Ohio Review* and edits *Quarter After Eight.* **(p. 137)**

Jon Munk is a poet and translator living in east-central Nebraska. His poetry has been published in *Prairie Schooner, Berkeley Poetry Review, Seneca Review, Plain Song Review,* and elsewhere. He has translated the complete poems of the nineteenth-century Spanish poet Gustavo Adolfo Bécquer and *Calle del Vento* by the late Italian poet Diego Valeri. **(p. 45)**

Jesse Nathan's poems have appeared in the *American Poetry Review, jubilat,* the *Nation,* the *Common Review,* the *Mennonite,* and many other magazines. He's a founding editor of the McSweeney's Poetry Series, and is at work on a PhD in English Literature at Stanford. In 2013, he was a fellow at the William Stafford Archives at Lewis & Clark College in Portland, Oregon. He lives some of the time in San Francisco's Mission District and some of the time in Menlo Park, down the peninsula. **(p. 29)**

Leonard Neufeldt is the author or editor/co-editor of sixteen books, most of them in literary or cultural history. But six of his volumes are collections of his poetry. His poems have appeared in virtually every major Canadian literary magazine, in leading literary serials throughout the U.S., and in numerous anthologies. Some of these poems have won awards, both in the U.S. and in Canada. **(p. 53)**

Ed Ochester's most recent book is *Unreconstructed: Poems Selected and New.* He is editor of the Pitt Poetry Series and one of the core faculty of the Bennington MFA Writing Seminars. Recent poems of his have appeared or are forthcoming in *American Poetry Review, Barrow Street, Agni, Boulevard,* etc. and *Best American Poetry 2013.* **(p. 58)**

Mary Rose O'Reilley's first book of poetry *Half Wild* won the 2005 Walt Whitman Award. Her second, *Earth, Mercy* came out in 2013. A teacher, potter, Quaker minister, farm worker and musician, she lives in Minnesota and tends some 200 species of herbs, fruit trees and berries on an urban homestead. "Renga" came out of a 4-month retreat on an island in Puget Sound, where, as part of discerning a new direction, she wrote haikus every morning. **(p. 31)**

William Palmer teaches English at Alma College in central Michigan. His poetry has recently appeared in *Ecotone, JAMA,* and *Salamander,* and he has published two chapbooks: *A String of Blue*

Lights (Pudding House) and *Humble* (Finishing Line). **(p. 134)**

Molly Peacock is a widely anthologized poet and writer. Her latest work of nonfiction is *The Paper Garden: Mrs. Delany Begins Her Life's Work at 72.* Her most recent collection of poems is *The Second Blush.* Always engaged with Stafford's idea of "revising your life," her next book is illustrated fiction, *Alphabetique: Tales in the Lives of the Letters.* **(p. 128)**

Joel Peckham is the author of three collections of poetry (*Movers and Shakers, The Heat of What Comes,* and *Nightwalking*) and a literary memoir, *Resisting Elegy: Essays on Grief and Recovery.* Poems and essays have appeared widely, including in *The Black Warrior Review, The North American Review, Prairie Schooner, River Teeth,* and *The Southern Review.* He lives with his wife Rachael and son Darius in Huntington, WV. **(p. 28)**

Oregon's sixth Poet Laureate, **Paulann Petersen** has five full-length books of poetry. A sixth, *Understory,* is forthcoming from Lost Horse Press in 2013. She was a Stegner Fellow at Stanford University and the recipient of the 2006 Holbrook Award from Oregon Literary Arts. She serves on the board of Friends of William Stafford, organizing the January Stafford Birthday Events. **(p. 21)**

Travis Poling has published poetry in *Alba, DreamSeeker,* and *CrossCurrents,* and in a self-published ebook, *Poems That Should Never be Read in Church.* He teaches college English composition in Richmond, Indiana. His recent Master's thesis in liturgical studies is based on Stafford's claim that "worship is poetry from beginning to end." Travis edits the *William Stafford Online Reader* at staffordreader.com. **(p. 105)**

Peter Quinn, a lifelong poet and businessperson, graduated from Lewis and Clark College where he studied with Vern Rutsala, Anthony Ostroff and, from the ages of 16-23, William Stafford. His book *Painting Circles on Straight Highways,* was published by Irenicon Press (2012). Quinn leads workshops at The Writers' Workshoppe, a writer-centric bookstore which he runs with his wife, Anna, in Port Townsend, Washington. **(p. 122)**

Kevin Rabas co-directs the creative writing program at Emporia State University and edits *Flint Hills Review*. He has four books: *Bird's Horn, Lisa's Flying Electric Piano* (a KS Notable Book and Nelson Poetry Book Award winner), *Sonny Kenner's Red Guitar*, and *Spider Face: stories.* (**p. 73**)

Mary Ellen Redmond earned her MFA from the Bennington Writing Seminars. Her poems have been published in *5am, The Drunken Boat, RATTLE, Primetime, Free State Review,* and *The Comstock Review*. She teaches English on Cape Cod, that hook-shaped peninsula that juts into the North Atlantic off the Massachusetts coast. (**p. 146**)

Shelley Reece taught literature and writing for forty-five years. He has also written essays and poems, sung with audition choirs, been a golf caddy, fish bait salesman, fly fisherman, bus boy, grocery sacker, dishwasher, marketing surveyor, construction worker, grain mill laborer, sewer worker, carpenter's assistant, and TV production crew member. He chaired the board for Friends of William Stafford from 2005-2010. (**p. 123**)

William Reyer is Professor of English at Heidelberg University in Tiffin, Ohio, where he has taught for thirty years. Among his teaching responsibilities are courses in creative writing. He is the author of *Promontory Pines: Poems* (2006). (**p. 103**)

Jack Ridl's latest collection is *Practicing to Walk Like a Heron* (Wayne State University Press.). He has also published *Broken Symmetry* (Wayne State) and *Losing Season* (CavanKerry). He is co-author with Peter Schakel of *Approaching Literature* (Bedford/St. Martin's). The Carnegie Foundation (CASE) named him Michigan's professor of the year. More than seventy-five of his students are now published authors. (**p. 50**)

Winner of *River Teeth's* 2012 Literary Non Fiction Book Prize (for *So Far, So Good*) and a Rockefeller Bellagio Award (poetry and fiction), **Ralph Salisbury** has published his thirteenth book, *Like the Sun in Storm* with Habit of Rainy Night's Press. It evokes his Native American heritage. *Light from a Bullet Hole*, Silverfish Review Press, was nominated for the Pulitzer Prize. (**p. 83**)

Derek Sheffield's book of poems *Through the Second Skin* was published in 2013 by Orchises Press. His work has appeared widely in literary journals such as *Poetry, Orion, The Georgia Review,* and *The Southern Review.* He lives with his family in the foothills of the Cascade Mountains near Leavenworth, Washington, and serves as poetry editor of *Terrain.org.* (**p. 89**)

William Sheldon lives with his family in Hutchinson, Kansas (birthplace of William Stafford), where he teaches and writes. His poetry and prose have appeared widely in small press publications. He is the author of three collections of poetry, *Retrieving Old Bones* (Woodley, 2002), *Into Distant Grass* (Oil Hill Press, 2009), and *Rain Comes Riding* (Mammoth, 2011). (**p. 62**)

Naomi Shihab Nye first met William Stafford at Notre Dame University at a literary festival in 1976, after loving his poems since high school. Later, he was generous enough to correspond with her, as he did with so many people, and she stayed friends with him till he died and with his whole family till now. (**p. 57**)

David Shumate is the author of three books of prose poetry, *High Water Mark* (2004), *The Floating Bridge* (2008), and *Kimonos in the Closet*, all published by the University of Pittsburgh Press. His poetry has also been anthologized in *The Best American Poetry, Good Poems for Hard Times, Writer's Almanac* and elsewhere. He lives in Zionsville, Indiana and teaches at Marian University. (**p. 33**)

Scot Siegel is a town planner from Oregon, where he lives with his wife and two daughters. His most recent book of poems is *Thousands Flee California Wildflowers* (Salmon Poetry). Siegel's poems appear in *High Desert Journal, Nimrod, Terrain.org, The Oregonian,* and *Verse Daily,* among other publications. (**p. 70**)

A lifetime member of the Friends of William Stafford, **Daniel Skach-Mills** is an award-winning poet, author, and a former Trappist monk. His books include *The Tao of Now* (Ken Arnold Books, 2008), *The Hut Beneath the Pine: Tea Poems* (a 2012 Oregon Book Award finalist) and *In This Forest of Monks* (2012). Daniel lives in Portland, Oregon. (**p. 120**)

Warren Slesinger graduated from the Iowa Writers Workshop in 1961 and taught English part-time while working full-time in the publishing business as an editor, marketing manager, and sales manager at the following university presses: Chicago, Oregon, Pennsylvania, and South Carolina. He has received an Ingram Merrill grant for writing (1971) and a South Carolina Poetry Fellowship (2003). **(p. 100)**

Thomas R. Smith's most recent books of poetry are *Waking Before Dawn*, and *The Foot of the Rainbow*, both from Red Dragonfly Press. He edited *Airmail: The Letters of Robert Bly and Tomas Tranströmer* (Graywolf Press) and teaches at the Loft Literary Center in Minneapolis. The first six lines of "Peace Vigil" are carved on a granite sculpture by Jill Sebastian at the Elizabeth Link Peace Park in Madison, Wisconsin. **(p. 85)**

Laura Smyth left years of urban existence behind for life on the remote Keweenaw Peninsula of Michigan. Her poetry is often inspired by the intersection of human nature and the natural world. She holds an MFA from Columbia University, has published in online and print journals and anthologies, and is a founding member of the Keweenaw Writers Workshop. **(p. 112)**

J.R. Solonche has been publishing poems in magazines, journals, and anthologies since the early '70s. He is coauthor of *Peach Girl: Poems for a Chinese Daughter* (Grayson Books) and author of the forthcoming *Beautiful Day* from Deerbrook Editions. He is a multiple nominee for Pushcart Prizes and the *Best of the Net* anthology. **(p. 139)**

Kim Stafford is the founding director of the Northwest Writing Institute at Lewis & Clark College and serves as literary executor for the Estate of William Stafford. He is the author of *100 Tricks Every Boy Can Do: How My Brother Disappeared* and *The Muses Among Us: Eloquent Listening and Other Pleasures of the Writer's Craft*. **(pp. 13, 127)**

David Stallings was born in the U.S. South, raised in Alaska and Colorado before settling in the Pacific Northwest. Once an academic geographer, he has long worked to promote public transportation in the Puget Sound area. His poems have appeared in several

North American and U.K. literary journals and anthologies, and in *Resurrection Bay*, a 2012 chapbook. **(p. 131)**

Scott T. Starbuck is a Creative Writing Coordinator at San Diego Mesa College. His most recent poetry book is *River Walker* (Mountains and Rivers Press, 2012). During his last sabbatical in 2006, he worked in the William Stafford Archives at Lewis and Clark College. He is a lifetime member of the Friends of William Stafford. **(p. 101)**

Doug Stone lives and writes in Albany, Oregon. He is a fourth generation Oregonian who, through poetry, is trying to unravel and understand the mysteries of this unique region he calls home. **(p. 65)**

Tim Suermondt is the author of two full-length collections: *Trying to Help the Elephant Dance* (The Backwaters Press, 2007) and *Just Beautiful* (New York Quarterly Books, 2010). His poems have appeared in *Poetry*, *The Georgia Review*, *Blackbird*, *Able Muse*, *Prairie Schooner*, *PANK*, *Bellevue Literary Review*, and elsewhere. He lives in Brooklyn with his wife, the poet Pui Ying Wong. **(p. 118)**

Arthur Sze is the author of eight books of poetry, including *The Ginkgo Light*, *Quipu*, *The Redshifting Web: Poems 1970-1998*, and *Archipelago*. A new collection, *Compass Rose*, is forthcoming from Copper Canyon Press in 2014. A professor emeritus at the Institute of American Indian Arts, he lives in Santa Fe, New Mexico. **(p. 71)**

Mark Thalman is the author of *Catching the Limit* (Fairweather Books, 2009) and editor of *poetry.us.com*. His work has been widely published for almost four decades, appearing in *Carolina Quarterly*, *CutBank*, *Pedestal Magazine*, and *Verse Daily*, among others. He received his MFA from the University of Oregon and has taught English in the public schools for thirty years. **(p. 42)**

Jeff Tigchelaar lives in Lawrence, Kansas. Recent poems appear or are forthcoming in *North American Review*, *Pleiades*, *CutBank*, *Flyway*, *Fugue*, *Best New Poets 2011*, *The Laurel Review*, *Coal City Review*, *Rhino*, *Gertrude*, *Garbanzo*, and *Verse Daily*. His blog, *Stay-at-Home Pop Culture*, is at xyztopeka.com. **(p. 140)**

Eric Torgersen's latest book is *Heart. Wood.* (Word Press 2012). His poems, translations and essays have appeared in *American Poetry Review, Hudson Review, Gettysburg Review, Field, Epoch, Pleiades, New Letters, New Ohio Review* and elsewhere. He retired in 2008 after teaching for thirty-eight years at Central Michigan University. **(p. 95)**

Wyatt Townley is the current Poet Laureate of Kansas. She has published five books, including *The Afterlives of Trees* (Woodley Press), *Perfectly Normal* (The Smith), and *The Breathing Field* (Little, Brown). Her work has been nominated for The Pushcart Prize, read by Garrison Keillor on NPR, featured by Ted Kooser in his syndicated column, and appeared in venues from *The Paris Review* to *Newsweek.* **(p. 150)**

Rosemerry Wahtola Trommer's poetry has appeared in *O Magazine*, in back alleys, on *A Prairie Home Companion* and in her children's lunch boxes. Her poetry collections include *The Less I Hold* and *The Miracle Already Happening: Everyday Life with Rumi.* She is a parent educator for Parents as Teachers. Favorite one-word mantra: *Adjust.* **(p. 98)**

Ken Waldman has six full-length poetry collections, a memoir, a children's book, and nine CDs that combine Appalachian-style string-band music with original poetry and Alaska-set storytelling. A former college professor, since 1995 he's worked as a freelance writer, musician, performer, and educator. **(p. 88)**

G.C. Waldrep's most recent books are *Your Father on the Train of Ghosts* (BOA Editions, 2011), a lyric collaboration with John Gallaher, and *The Arcadia Project: North American Postmodern Pastoral* (Ahsahta, 2012), an anthology co-edited with Joshua Corey. He teaches at Bucknell University, edits the journal *West Branch*, and serves as Editor-at-Large for *The Kenyon Review.* **(p. 56)**

Connie Wanek is the author of three books of poetry, most recently *On Speaking Terms* from Copper Canyon Press (2010). Her work has appeared in *Poetry, The Atlantic Monthly*, and many other journals. **(p. 96)**

Sarah Webb has recently retired after twelve years as Poetry and Fiction Editor for *Crosstimbers*, the multidisciplinary journal of the

University of Science and Arts of Oklahoma. She continues to co-edit the online Zen arts magazine *Just This*. Her poetry collection *Black* is forthcoming from Virtual Arts Collective. **(p. 126)**

Ingrid Wendt's first book of poems, *Moving the House*, was selected by William Stafford for BOA Editions' New Poets of America Series. Subsequent books have won the Oregon Book Award, the Yellowglen Award, and the Editions Prize. Her newest book, *Evensong*, is available from Truman State University Press. With her husband, writer Ralph Salisbury, she lives in Eugene, Oregon. **(p. 66)**

David Whyte makes his home in the Pacific Northwest, where rain and changeable skies remind him of his other, more distant homes: Yorkshire, Wales, and Ireland. He travels and lectures throughout the world, bringing his own and others' poetry to large audiences. He is an Associate Fellow of Saïd at the University of Oxford. **(p. 116)**

Paul Willis is professor of English at Westmont College and a former Poet Laureate of Santa Barbara. His most recent collections of poetry are *Rosing from the Dead* (WordFarm) and *Visiting Home* (Pecan Grove Press). Since 2007, he has hosted an annual community reading of Stafford's poems on the site of Los Prietos Civilian Public Service camp, where Stafford and many other conscientious objectors did alternative service during WWII. **(p. 81)**

Patricia Wixon's 2011 chapbook *Airing the Sheets* was published by Finishing Line Press. She helped form Friends of William Stafford and was its first board president. Since her retirement from public education, she has volunteered in the William Stafford Archives and produced ninety-seven CD recordings of William Stafford's readings, workshops, and interviews spanning forty years. **(p. 91)**

Vincent Wixon's most recent book of poems is *Blue Moon: Poems from Chinese Lines* from Wordcraft of Oregon. He coproduced two videos on William Stafford, and, with former Director of the William Stafford Archives Paul Merchant, edited Stafford's *Crossing Unmarked Snow* and *The Answers Are Inside the Mountains*, both published by University of Michigan Press. Their latest collaboration is a book of Stafford's aphorisms and aphoristic poems, to be published in the Pitt Poetry Series in early 2014. **(p. 25)**

Permissions &
Acknowledgments

We are grateful to the authors who have given permission to include previously published work in this anthology. We also thank the editors and publishers who have given us permission to reprint poems.

Tim Barnes, "Kansas, Maybe." Originally published in *The Friends of William Stafford Newsletter*. Reprinted by permission of the author.

Ellen Bass, "The Muse of Work." First published in *New Ohio Review* (Spring 2012). Reprinted by permission of the author.

Claire Bateman, "One Morning We'll All Awaken without a Theory." First published in *The Curator*. Reprinted by permission of the author.

Marvin Bell, "With Stafford at Centrum," from *Annie-Over*, Honeybrook Press, 1988. Copyright © 1988 by Marvin Bell. Reprinted by permission of the author.

Jaswinder Bolina, "The Last National," first appeared in *Explosion-Proof Magazine* (Issue 5). Reprinted by permission of the author.

Emily K. Bright, "At the State Correctional Facility," from *Come Together: Imagine Peace*, Bottom Dog Press, 2008. Used with permission of the author.

Margaret Chula, "Equilibrium," from *What Remains: Japanese Americans in Internment Camps* (Katsura Press). Reprinted by permission of the author.

David Citino, "Charms Against Writer's Block," from *The Discipline: New and Selected Poems, 1980-1992* (The Ohio State University Press). Reprinted with permission from Mary Citino.

Philip Dacey, "Telling William Stafford's Ghost Why I Moved to New York City," previously appeared in *Skidrow Penthouse*. Reprinted by permission of the author.

In "From My Daddy Who Could Not Be Here Today" by Betty Davis, "sometimes the whole world leans against you" nods to William Stafford's line, "Sometimes whole sides of the world / lean against where you live" from the poem "Home State" (*The Way It Is:*

New & Selected Poems, Graywolf Press).

Todd Davis, "In a Dream William Stafford Visits Me" first appeared in *Image.* Reprinted with permission from the author.

James Dickson, "In Peace." First published in *Evening Street Review* (March 2013). Reprinted by permission of the author.

Sarah Estes, "Ars Poetica." First appeared in *Lalitamba* in a slightly altered version titled "Ultimate Telos." Reprinted by permission of the author.

Helen Frost, "That Certainty," from *as if a dry wind* published by Pecan Grove Press, 2009. Reprinted by permission of the author.

Charles Goodrich, "Daoist Out of Kansas," from *A Scripture of Crows* (Silverfish Review Press, 2013). Reprinted by permission of the author.

Kathleen Gunton, "The Message & William Stafford: Cento." First published in *Perceptions: A Magazine of the Arts* (May 2013). Reprinted by permission of the author.

Patrick Hicks, "Burqa." Originally appeared in the *Christian Science Monitor* and his book *This London* (Salmon Poetry, 2010). Reprinted by permission of the author.

Chloe Honum, "Evening News." First published in *Linebreak.* Reprinted by permission of the author.

Joan Houlihan, "Rationing, 1945," from *The Mending Worm.* Copyright © 2006 by Joan Houlihan. Used by permission of New Issues Poetry & Prose.

Meg Hutchinson, "Don't Wait," from *The Morning I Was Born* (LRH Music and Productions, 2012) and inspired by a poetry prompt from her mom, Janet Hutchinson, using Stafford's quotes. Reprinted by permission of the author.

Joseph Hutchison, "The Map," from *House of Mirrors,* James Andrews & Co., Inc., 1992. Reprinted by permission of the author.

as a broadside by Paper Crane Press to commemorate his retirement from the William Stafford Archives. Reprinted by permission of the author.

Caryn Mirriam-Goldberg, "Talking to Stafford Late at Night," from *Kansas Poems of William Stafford,* 2nd edition, edited by Denise Low, Woodley Press. Reprinted by permission of the author.

Brad Modlin, "What You Missed That Day You Were Absent from Fourth Grade." First appeared in *The Pinch*. Reprinted by permission of the author.

A different version of Jesse Nathan's "What Do You Really Believe" appeared in *Dinner* (Milk Machine, 2009), a chapbook of his poems set to music by Chris Janzen. Reprinted by permission of the author.

Leonard Neufeldt, "Letter to Bill Stafford," from *Yarrow*, Black Moss Press, 1993. Copyright © Leonard Neufeldt. Reprinted with permission from the author.

Ed Ochester, "In Praise of William Stafford," from *Unreconstructed: Poems Selected and New*, Autumn House Press. Copyright © 2007 by Ed Ochester. Reprinted by permission of the author.

Mary Rose O'Reilley, "Renga." First published in *Wisdom Ways: A Ministry of the Sisters of St. Joseph of Carondelet* (January/May 2013) 12. Reprinted by permission of the author.

William Palmer, "Low Standards." First published in *College Composition and Communication*, Vol. 43, No. 4, Dec. 1992. Reprinted by permission of the author.

Molly Peacock, "The Analyst Draws." First published in the online series *A Poetry Congeries* housed at *Connotation Press: An Online Artifact* (June 2013). Reprinted by permission of the author.

Paulann Petersen, "From the Very Start," *Understory*, Lost Horse Press, 2013. Reprinted by permission of the author.

Travis Poling, "Some Beliefs About Mountains," from *Poems That Should Never be Read in Church*, Ghost Cat Press, 2010. Reprinted

CPSIA information can be obtained at www.ICGtesting.com
Printed in the USA
LVOW11s1924050114

368162LV00001BA/3/P

9 780985 458683